Studio

AQA GCSE French
Higher
Vocabulary Book

P Pearson

Published by Pearson Education Limited, 80 Strand, London, WC2R 0RL
www.pearsonschoolsandfecolleges.co.uk
Text © Pearson Education Limited 2017
Editorial management by Gwladys Rushworth for Haremi
Edited by Fabienne Tartarin
Typeset by York Publishing Solutions Pvt. Ltd.
Cover image: Alamy Images: kevers
Cover © Pearson Education Limited 2017

Written by Angela Stanley

First published 2017
10 9 8 7 6 5 4 3 2

British Library Cataloguing in Publication Data
A catalogue record for this book is available from the British Library.
ISBN 978 1 292 13242 6

Copyright notice
All rights reserved. No part of this publication may be reproduced in any form or by any means (including photocopying or storing it in any medium by electronic means and whether or not transiently or incidentally to some other use of this publication) without the written permission of the copyright owner, except in accordance with the provisions of the Copyright, Design and Patents Act 1988 or under the terms of a license issued by the Copyright Licensing Agency, Barnard's Inn, 86 Fetter Lane, London EC4A 1EN (www.cla.co.uk). Applications for the copyright owner's written permission should be addressed to the publisher.

Printed in the UK by Ashford Colour Press

Contenu

High-frequency words **4**

Module 1
Words I should know for speaking and writing activities **15**
Extra words I should know for reading and listening activities **18**

Module 2
Words I should know for speaking and writing activities **19**
Extra words I should know for reading and listening activities **22**

Module 3
Words I should know for speaking and writing activities **23**
Extra words I should know for reading and listening activities **26**

Module 4
Words I should know for speaking and writing activities **27**
Extra words I should know for reading and listening activities **30**

Module 5
Words I should know for speaking and writing activities **31**
Extra words I should know for reading and listening activities **34**

Module 6
Words I should know for speaking and writing activities **35**
Extra words I should know for reading and listening activities **38**

Module 7
Words I should know for speaking and writing activities **39**
Extra words I should know for reading and listening activities **42**

Module 8
Words I should know for speaking and writing activities **43**
Extra words I should know for reading and listening activities **46**

High-frequency words

Common –er verbs

accepter	to accept
adorer	to love, to adore
aider	to help
aimer	to like
aller	to go
aller à pied	to walk
allumer	to light, to turn, to switch on
améliorer	to improve
(s)'arrêter	to stop

Had a look ☐ **Nearly there** ☐ **Nailed it** ☐

chanter	to sing
chercher	to look for
cliquer	to click (ICT)
coller	to stick
commander	to order
compter/compter sur	to count, to intend, to count on (someone)
contacter	to contact
continuer	to continue, to carry on
copier	to copy
se coucher	to go to bed
coûter	to cost

Had a look ☐ **Nearly there** ☐ **Nailed it** ☐

se débrouiller	to cope, to manage, to get by
décider	to decide
décoller	to take off (plane)
se dépêcher	to hurry
dépenser	to spend (money)
se déshabiller	to get undressed
désirer	to want, to desire
dessiner	to draw
détester	to hate
discuter	to discuss
donner	to give
durer	to last

Had a look ☐ **Nearly there** ☐ **Nailed it** ☐

s'échapper	to escape
écouter	to listen
écraser	to squash
empêcher	to prevent
endommager	to harm, to damage
entrer	to enter, to go in
envoyer	to send
espérer	to hope
essayer	to try
étudier	to study
expliquer	to explain

Had a look ☐ **Nearly there** ☐ **Nailed it** ☐

se fâcher	to get angry
fermer	to close, to switch off
frapper	to knock, to hit
gagner	to earn, to win
garder	to look after, to mind (child, dog)
garer	to park
gérer	to manage (business)
s'habiller	to get dressed
habiter	to live (inhabit)
informer	to inform
inviter	to invite
jeter	to throw

Had a look ☐ **Nearly there** ☐ **Nailed it** ☐

laisser	to leave behind (an object)
(se) laver	to wash
se lever	to get up
louer	to rent, to hire
manger	to eat
manquer	to miss, to be lacking
marcher	to walk, to work (function)
mériter	to deserve
monter	to climb, to get on(to), to go up
monter (dans)	to get into (bus, car, train)
montrer	to show
nettoyer	to clean
noter	to note

Had a look ☐ **Nearly there** ☐ **Nailed it** ☐

s'occuper de	to look after
organiser	to organise
ôter	to take off (clothes etc.)
oublier	to forget, to leave something behind
pardonner	to forgive
parler	to speak
passer	to pass, to spend (time)
penser	to think (about)
peser	to weigh
pleurer	to cry
porter	to wear
poser	to place
pousser	to push
préférer	to prefer

High-frequency words

présenter	to introduce (a person), to present
prêter	to lend
se promener	to go for a walk
quitter	to leave (somewhere, somebody)

Had a look ☐ **Nearly there** ☐ **Nailed it** ☐

raconter	to tell, to recount
se rappeler	to remember
rater	to fail, to miss (train, bus, etc.)
rechercher	to research
recommander	to recommend
regretter	to regret, to be sorry
rembourser	to refund
remercier	to thank
remplacer	to replace
rencontrer	to meet
rentrer (à la maison)	to return (home), to go back (home)
renverser	to knock over
réparer	to repair
répéter	to repeat
se reposer	to rest
réserver	to reserve
ressembler	to look like, to resemble
rester	to stay
retourner (à l'école)	to return (to school), to go back (to school)
se réveiller	to wake up
rouler	to go (in a car)

Had a look ☐ **Nearly there** ☐ **Nailed it** ☐

sauter	to jump
sauver	to save
sembler	to seem
signer	to sign
signifier	to mean, to signify
sonner	to ring (a bell)
souhaiter	to wish
stationner	to park
téléphoner	to phone
(se) terminer	to end
tirer	to pull
tomber	to fall
toucher	to touch
travailler	to work
traverser	to cross, to go across
trouver	to find
utiliser	to use
vérifier	to check
voler	to fly, to steal
voyager	to travel

Had a look ☐ **Nearly there** ☐ **Nailed it** ☐

Common –ir verbs

atterrir	to land
choisir	to choose
s'endormir	to fall asleep
finir	to finish, to end
nourrir	to feed, to nourish
offrir	to offer, to give a present/gift
ouvrir	to open
partir	to leave, to depart
prévenir	to warn
remplir	to fill, to fill in
réussir	to succeed
se servir de	to use
sortir	to go out
se souvenir	to remember
tenir	to hold
venir	to come

Had a look ☐ **Nearly there** ☐ **Nailed it** ☐

Common –re verbs

apprendre	to learn
attendre	to wait for
boire	to drink
conduire	to drive
connaître	to know (person, place)
décrire	to describe
descendre (de)	to get out of (bus, car, train)
dire	to tell, to say
entendre	to hear
éteindre	to switch off
(se) faire mal	to hurt (oneself)
introduire	to introduce (an item, an idea)
lire	to read

Had a look ☐ **Nearly there** ☐ **Nailed it** ☐

mettre	to put
plaire (à)	to please
prendre	to take
produire	to produce
remettre	to put back
répondre	to reply
rire	to laugh
sourire	to smile

High-frequency words

suivre	to follow
vivre	to live
vendre	to sell

Had a look ☐ **Nearly there** ☐ **Nailed it** ☐

Common –oir verbs

avoir	to have
avoir besoin de	to need
avoir l'intention de (faire)	to mean to (do)
devoir	to have to, must
savoir	to know (a fact)
voir	to see
vouloir	to want

Had a look ☐ **Nearly there** ☐ **Nailed it** ☐

Common adjectives: describing someone

actif/-ve	active
agréable	pleasant
amical(e)	friendly
bavard(e)	talkative
bête	silly
calme	peaceful, quiet, calm
désagréable	unpleasant
drôle	funny (comical)
égoïste	selfish
généreux/-euse	generous
gentil(le)	kind
gros(se)	fat
honnête	honest
indépendant(e)	independent
intelligent(e)	intelligent, clever
joli(e)	pretty
laid(e)	ugly
marrant(e)	funny (comical)
méchant(e)	naughty
mince	slim

Had a look ☐ **Nearly there** ☐ **Nailed it** ☐

moche	ugly
mûr(e)	mature
optimiste	optimistic
paresseux/-euse	lazy
(im)patient(e)	(im)patient
pessimiste	pessimistic
petit(e)	small, short (person)
(im)poli(e)	(im)polite
populaire	popular
responsable	responsible
rigolo(te)	funny (comical)
sage	good (well-behaved), wise
sérieux/-euse	serious
sévère	strict
strict(e)	strict
sympa (invariable)	nice, likeable
sympathique	nice, likeable
timide	shy
travailleur/-euse	hard-working
vilain(e)	naughty

Had a look ☐ **Nearly there** ☐ **Nailed it** ☐

Common adjectives: I am, you are, we are ...

célèbre	famous
content(e)	pleased
de bonne humeur	in a good mood
étonné(e)	surprised
faible (en maths, etc.)	weak (in maths, etc.)
fatigué(e)	tired
fort(e) (en maths, etc.)	strong (in maths, etc.)
heureux/-euse	happy, content
inquiet/-iète	worried
jeune	young
malheureux/-euse	unhappy
perdu(e)	lost
pressé(e)	in a hurry
reconnaissant(e)	grateful
riche	rich
satisfait(e)	satisfied
sauf/-ve	safe
surpris(e)	surprised
triste	sad
vieux/vieil/vieille	old

Had a look ☐ **Nearly there** ☐ **Nailed it** ☐

Common adjectives: opinions

amusant(e)	fun, amusing
bruyant(e)	noisy
cher/-ère	expensive
chouette	great (fantastic)
démodé(e)	old fashioned
dur(e)	hard
effrayant(e)	frightening
facile	easy, simple
fantastique	fantastic
fatigant(e)	tiring
favori(te)	favourite
formidable	great (marvellous)
génial(e)	great (fantastic)
idéal(e)	ideal
incroyable	unbelievable

High-frequency words

injuste	*unfair*
inutile	*useless*
juste	*fair*

Had a look ☐ Nearly there ☐ Nailed it ☐

magnifique	*magnificent*
malsain(e)	*unhealthy*
merveilleux/-euse	*marvellous*
nécessaire	*necessary*
négatif/-ve	*negative*
parfait(e)	*perfect*
passionnant(e)	*exciting*
positif/-ve	*positive*
pratique	*practical*
préféré(e)	*favourite*
raisonnable	*reasonable*
ridicule	*ridiculous*
sain(e)	*healthy (food/way of life)*
sensationnel(le)	*sensational*
sensass	*sensational*
simple	*easy, simple*
super	*great (fantastic)*
superbe	*superb*
utile	*useful*
valable	*valid*
vrai(e)	*true*

Had a look ☐ Nearly there ☐ Nailed it ☐

Other common adjectives

à la mode	*fashionable*
ancien(ne)	*former, old*
autre	*other*
chaud(e)	*hot*
court(e)	*short*
d'une grande valeur	*valuable*
dernier/-ière	*last*
étroit(e)	*thin, narrow*
fermé à clef	*locked*
grand(e)	*large, big*
gratuit(e)	*free (at no cost)*
grave	*serious*
gros(se)	*large, big*
haut(e)	*high, tall (building)*
léger/-ère	*light*
libre	*free (unoccupied, available)*
long(ue)	*long*
lourd(e)	*heavy*

Had a look ☐ Nearly there ☐ Nailed it ☐

même	*same*
moderne	*modern*
mouillé(e)	*wet*
mûr(e)	*ripe*
neuf/-ve	*new (brand new)*
nombreux/-euse	*numerous*
normal(e)	*normal*
nouveau/nouvel/nouvelle	*new*
ouvert(e)	*open*

Had a look ☐ Nearly there ☐ Nailed it ☐

pareil(le)	*alike, the same*
plein(e)	*full*
pourri(e)	*rotten*
prêt(e)	*ready*
prochain(e)	*next*
propre	*own*
rangé(e)	*tidy*
rapide	*fast*
récent(e)	*recent*
reconnu(e)	*recognised, well known*
réel(le)	*real*
silencieux/-ieuse	*silent*
situé(e)	*situated*
tranquille	*peaceful, quiet, calm*
type	*typical*

Had a look ☐ Nearly there ☐ Nailed it ☐

Comparisons/Superlatives

plus/moins	*more/less*
plus que/moins que	*more than/less than*
bon/meilleur/le meilleur	*good/better/best*
mauvais/pire/le pire	*bad/worse/worst*
bien/mieux/le mieux	*well/better/best*
mal/plus mal/le plus mal	*badly/worse/worst*
beaucoup/plus/le plus	*a lot, lots/more/the most*
peu/moins/le moins	*few, little/less/the least*

Had a look ☐ Nearly there ☐ Nailed it ☐

Common adverbs

à peine	*hardly*
assez	*fairly, quite*
aussi	*too, as well*
trop	*too*
bien	*well*
bientôt	*soon*
bon marché	*cheap(ly)*
d'habitude	*usually*
debout	*standing*
déjà	*already*
encore	*again*
ensemble	*together*

High-frequency words

fort	loud(ly)	contre	against
(mal)heureusement	(un)fortunately	dans	in (inside)
ici	here	de	from
immédiatement	immediately	dehors	outside
jamais	never	**Had a look** ☐ **Nearly there** ☐ **Nailed it** ☐	
là	there	depuis	since, for
là-bas	over there	derrière	behind
là-haut	up there	devant	in front of, in the front
longtemps	(for) a long time	en	in, within (time)
Had a look ☐ **Nearly there** ☐ **Nailed it** ☐		en dehors de	outside (of)
normalement	usually	en face de	opposite
nulle part	nowhere	en haut	above
partout	everywhere	en-dessous	under/underneath
pas encore	not yet	entre	between
peut-être	perhaps	jusqu'à	until
plutôt	rather	loin de	far from
presque	almost	malgré	despite, in spite of
quelque part	somewhere	nulle part	nowhere
quelquefois	sometimes	par	through
rarement	rarely	parmi	among(st)
récemment	recently	pour	for, in order to
souvent	often	près (de)	near (to)
surtout	especially	sans	without
toujours	always, still	selon	according to
tout de suite	straight away, immediately	sous	under/underneath
très	very	sur	on (on top of)
vite	quickly	vers	towards
vraiment	really	**Had a look** ☐ **Nearly there** ☐ **Nailed it** ☐	
Had a look ☐ **Nearly there** ☐ **Nailed it** ☐			

Prepositions

Connectives

à	at, to	à cause de	because of
à côté de	next to	à part	apart from
à partir de	from	ainsi	so, therefore
à travers	across	alors	so, therefore, then
après	after	aussi	also
au bord de	at the side/edge of	car	because
au bout de	at the end of	cependant	however
au fond	in the background, at the back	c'est-à-dire	that is to say, i.e.
au fond de	at the back of, at the bottom of	comme	as, like
au lieu de	instead of	d'un côté/de l'autre côté	on the one hand/on the other hand
au milieu (de)	in the middle (of)	donc	so, therefore
au premier plan	in the foreground	**Had a look** ☐ **Nearly there** ☐ **Nailed it** ☐	
au-dessus de	above	ensuite	next
autour de	around	évidemment	obviously
avant	before	mais	but
avec	with	même si	even if
chez	at (someone's house)	ou	or
		par contre	on the other hand

High-frequency words

par exemple	for example
pendant que	while
pourtant	however
puis	then
puisque	seeing that, since
quand	when
sans doute	undoubtedly, without doubt, probably
si	if
y compris	including

Had a look ☐ **Nearly there** ☐ **Nailed it** ☐

Numbers

un(e)	1
deux	2
trois	3
quatre	4
cinq	5
six	6
sept	7
huit	8
neuf	9
dix	10
onze	11
douze	12
treize	13
quatorze	14
quinze	15
seize	16
dix-sept	17
dix-huit	18
dix-neuf	19

Had a look ☐ **Nearly there** ☐ **Nailed it** ☐

vingt	20
vingt et un	21
vingt-deux	22
vingt-trois	23
vingt-quatre	24
vingt-cinq	25
vingt-six	26
vingt-sept	27
vingt-huit	28
vingt-neuf	29
trente	30
trente et un	31
trente-deux, etc.	32, etc.
quarante	40
cinquante	50
soixante	60

Had a look ☐ **Nearly there** ☐ **Nailed it** ☐

soixante-dix	70
soixante et onze	71
soixante-douze	72
soixante-treize	73
soixante-quatorze	74
soixante-quinze	75
soixante-seize	76
soixante-dix-sept	77
soixante-dix-huit	78
soixante-dix-neuf	79

Had a look ☐ **Nearly there** ☐ **Nailed it** ☐

quatre-vingts	80
quatre-vingt-un	81
quatre-vingt-deux, etc.	82, etc.
quatre-vingt-dix	90
quatre-vingt-onze	91
quatre-vingt-douze, etc.	92, etc.

Had a look ☐ **Nearly there** ☐ **Nailed it** ☐

cent (m)	100
cent un(e)	101
cent vingt	120
deux cents	200
mille (m)	1000
mille cent	1100
deux mille	2000
un million (m)	1,000,000
deux millions (m)	2,000,000
premier/-ière	first
deuxième	second
onzième	eleventh
vingt-et-unième	twenty -first

Had a look ☐ **Nearly there** ☐ **Nailed it** ☐

Opinions

à mon avis	in my opinion
absolument	absolutely
bien entendu	of course
bien sûr	of course
ça dépend	that depends
ça m'énerve	it gets on my nerves
ça me fait rire	it makes me laugh
ça me plaît	I like it
ça m'est égal	it's all the same to me
ça ne me dit rien	it means nothing to me, I don't fancy that, I don't feel like it
ça suffit	that's enough
ça ne fait rien	it doesn't matter
ce n'est pas la peine	it's not worth it

High-frequency words

d'accord	OK (in agreement)
j'en ai assez/marre	I've had enough
personnellement	personally

Had a look ☐ **Nearly there** ☐ **Nailed it** ☐

Other useful expressions

à bientôt	see you soon
à demain/vendredi	see you tomorrow/on Friday
bonne chance	good luck
bon courage	good luck
Ça s'écrit comment?	How do you spell that?
ça va	I'm fine, it's OK
comme çi, comme ça	so-so
désolé(e)	sorry
défense de	you are not allowed to
dommage	what a shame
excuse-/excusez-moi	(I'm) sorry (informal/formal)
il est interdit de	you are not allowed to

Had a look ☐ **Nearly there** ☐ **Nailed it** ☐

il faut	you must/one must
il y a	there is/are
je ne comprends pas	I don't understand
je ne sais pas	I don't know
merci (bien)	thank you (very much)
Qu'est-ce que cela veut dire?	What does that mean?
avec plaisir	with pleasure
tant mieux	all/so much the better
tant pis	too bad
voici	here is/are
voilà	there is/are (i.e. over there)
volontiers	with pleasure

Had a look ☐ **Nearly there** ☐ **Nailed it** ☐

Other useful little words

ça/cela	that
le chiffre	figure (number)
la chose	thing
comme	as, like
la façon	way (manner)
la fois	time (occasion)
le genre	type (kind of)
madame	Mrs, Madam
mademoiselle	Miss
monsieur	Mr, Sir
le nombre	number
le numéro	number (phone number)
par exemple	for example

quelqu'un	someone
quelque chose	something
sauf	except
la sorte	type (kind of)
tout le monde	everybody

Had a look ☐ **Nearly there** ☐ **Nailed it** ☐

Time, frequency and sequencing expressions

à … heure(s)	at … o'clock
à … heure(s) et quart	at quarter past …
à … heure(s) et demie	at half past …
à … heure(s) moins le quart	at quarter to …
à la fois	at the same time
à l'avenir	in future, from now on
à l'heure	on time
à temps partiel	part-time
l'an (m)	year
l'année (f)	year
après	after
après-demain	the day after tomorrow
après-midi	afternoon
aujourd'hui	today
auparavant	formerly, in the past
avant	before
avant-hier	the day before yesterday
bientôt	soon

Had a look ☐ **Nearly there** ☐ **Nailed it** ☐

d'abord	at first, firstly
dans le futur	in the future
d'habitude	usually
de bonne heure	early
le début	start
demain	tomorrow
dernier/-ière	last
de temps en temps	from time to time
déjà	already
de nouveau	again
en attendant	whilst waiting (for), meanwhile
en avance	in advance
en ce moment	at the moment
en retard	late
en train de (faire…)	(to be) doing
en même temps	at the same time
encore une fois	once more, again
enfin	at last, finally
environ	about, approximately

Had a look ☐ **Nearly there** ☐ **Nailed it** ☐

High-frequency words

la fin	end	Quel/Quelle?	What/Which?
hier	yesterday	Quand?	When?
il y a	ago	Où?	Where?
le jour	day	Lequel/Laquelle/	Which one(s)?
la journée	day	Lesquels/Lesquelles?	
le lendemain	the next day	Qui?	Who?
longtemps	for a long time	Pourquoi?	Why?
maintenant	now		

Had a look ☐ Nearly there ☐ Nailed it ☐

le matin	morning
le mois	month
normalement	normally
la nuit	night
parfois	sometimes
le passé	past
pendant	during
plus tard	later
presque	almost, nearly
prochain	next

Colours

blanc(he)	white
bleu(e)	blue
brun(e)	brown
châtain (invariable)	chestnut brown
clair(e)	light
foncé(e)	dark
gris(e)	grey
jaune	yellow
marron (invariable)	brown, chestnut brown
noir(e)	black
rose	pink
rouge	red
vert(e)	green
violet(te)	violet

Had a look ☐ Nearly there ☐ Nailed it ☐

quelquefois	sometimes
rarement	rarely
récemment	recently
la semaine	week
seulement	only
le siècle	century
le soir	evening
soudain	suddenly
souvent	often
suivant	following
sur le point de (être)	(to be) about to
tard	late
tôt	early
toujours	always, still
tous les jours	every day
tout à coup	suddenly, all of a sudden
tout de suite	immediately
vite	quickly

Had a look ☐ Nearly there ☐ Nailed it ☐

Had a look ☐ Nearly there ☐ Nailed it ☐

Days, months and seasons of the year

lundi	Monday
mardi	Tuesday
mercredi	Wednesday
jeudi	Thursday
vendredi	Friday
samedi	Saturday
dimanche	Sunday

Had a look ☐ Nearly there ☐ Nailed it ☐

le mois	month
janvier	January
février	February
mars	March
avril	April
mai	May
juin	June
juillet	July
août	August
septembre	September
octobre	October
novembre	November
décembre	December

Had a look ☐ Nearly there ☐ Nailed it ☐

Question words

Comment?	How?
Combien (de)?	How much, How many?
Que?	What?
Qu'est-ce qui?	What? (as subject)
Qu'est-ce que?	What? (as object)
Quoi?	What?
De quelle couleur?	What colour?
Comment?	What like?
À quelle heure?	(At) what time?

High-frequency words

la saison	season
(au) printemps (m)	(in) spring
(en) été (m)	(in) summer
(en) automne (m)	(in) autumn
(en) hiver (m)	(in) winter

Had a look ☐ **Nearly there** ☐ **Nailed it** ☐

Quantities and measures

assez (de)	enough
beaucoup (de)	a lot (of), many
un centilitre	centilitre
un centimètre	centimetre
demi	half
une gramme	gramme
un kilomètre	kilometre
un mètre	metre
moins (de)	less
encore (de)	(some) more
pas mal (de)	quite a few
(un) peu (de)	a little of, few
plus (de)	more
plusieurs	several
le poids	weight
la quantité	quantity
un quart	quarter
quelques	some
un tiers	third
trop (de)	too much, too many

Had a look ☐ **Nearly there** ☐ **Nailed it** ☐

un kilo (de)	a kilo (of)
un litre (de)	a litre (of)
un morceau (de)	a piece (of)
un paquet (de)	a packet (of)
un peu (de)	a little (of)
un pot (de)	a jar (of)
une boîte (de)	a tin (of), a box (of)
une bouteille (de)	a bottle (of)
une centaine (de)	about a hundred
une douzaine (de)	a dozen
une tranche (de)	a slice (of)
une vingtaine (de)	about twenty

Had a look ☐ **Nearly there** ☐ **Nailed it** ☐

Countries

l'Algérie (f)	Algeria
l'Allemagne (f)	Germany
l'Angleterre (f)	England
l'Autriche (f)	Austria
la Belgique	Belgium
le Canada	Canada
la Chine	China
le Danemark	Denmark
la France	France
la Grande-Bretagne	Great Britain
la Grèce	Greece
la Hollande	Holland

Had a look ☐ **Nearly there** ☐ **Nailed it** ☐

l'Inde (f)	India
l'Irlande (f)	Ireland
l'Italie (f)	Italy
les Pays-Bas (m)	Netherlands
le Pakistan	Pakistan
la Russie	Russia
l'Écosse (f)	Scotland
le Sénégal	Senegal
l'Espagne (f)	Spain
la Suisse	Switzerland
la Tunisie	Tunisia
la Turquie	Turkey
le Royaume-Uni	United Kingdom
les États-Unis (m)	United States
le pays de Galles	Wales

Had a look ☐ **Nearly there** ☐ **Nailed it** ☐

Continents

l'Afrique (f)	Africa
l'Asie (f)	Asia
l'Australie (f)	Australia
l'Europe (f)	Europe
l'Amérique du Nord (f)	North America
l'Amérique du Sud (f)	South America

Had a look ☐ **Nearly there** ☐ **Nailed it** ☐

Nationalities

algérien(ne)	Algerian
allemand(e)	German
américain(e)	American
anglais(e)	English
autrichien(ne)	Austrian
belge	Belgian
britannique	British
canadien(ne)	Canadian
chinois(e)	Chinese
corse	Corsican
danois(e)	Danish
écossais(e)	Scottish
espagnol(e)	Spanish
européen(ne)	European

High-frequency words

français(e)	French	le bois	wood
gallois(e)	Welsh	le cuir	leather
grec(que)	Greek	le fer	iron
hollandais(e)	Dutch	la laine	wool

Had a look ☐ **Nearly there** ☐ **Nailed it** ☐

		l'or (m)	gold
indien(ne)	Indian	la soie	silk
irlandais(e)	Irish	le verre	glass
italien(ne)	Italian		

Had a look ☐ **Nearly there** ☐ **Nailed it** ☐

pakistanais(e)	Pakistani		
russe	Russian	**Climate**	
suisse	Swiss	l'averse (f)	shower
tunisien(ne)	Tunisian	briller	to shine
turque	Turkish	le brouillard	fog

Had a look ☐ **Nearly there** ☐ **Nailed it** ☐

		la brume	mist
Geographical surroundings		la chaleur	heat
à droite	on/to the right	le ciel	sky
à gauche	on/to the left	le climat	climate
chez	at the house of	couvert	overcast
de chaque côté	from each side	doux	mild
de l'autre côté	from the other side	l'éclair (m)	lightning
en bas	down(stairs)	l'éclaircie (f)	bright spell
en haut	up(stairs)	ensoleillé	sunny
ici	here	faire beau	to be fine (weather)
là	there	faire mauvais	to be bad (weather)
là-bas	over there	geler	to freeze
la banlieue	suburb	la glace	ice
la campagne	countryside	humide	humid, wet
le centre-ville	town centre	la météo	weather forecast
la ville	town	mouillé	wet

Had a look ☐ **Nearly there** ☐ **Nailed it** ☐

		neiger	to snow
loin de	far from	le nuage	cloud
nulle part	nowhere	nuageux	cloudy
par	by	l'ombre (f)	shade, shadow
partout	everywhere	l'orage (m)	storm
quelque part	somewhere	orageux	stormy
situé(e)	situated	pleuvoir	to rain
tout droit	straight ahead	la pluie	rain
tout près	very near	sec	dry
toutes directions	all directions	la tempête	storm
l'est (m)	east	le temps	weather
l'ouest (m)	west	le tonnerre	thunder
le nord	north	tremper	to soak
le sud	south	le vent	wind

Had a look ☐ **Nearly there** ☐ **Nailed it** ☐

Social conventions

à plus tard	see you later
à tout à l'heure	see you later

Materials

l'argent (m)	silver
le béton	concrete

High-frequency words

allô	*hello (on the telephone)*
amitiés	*best wishes*
amuse-toi/amusez-vous bien!	*enjoy yourself/yourselves!*
au revoir	*goodbye*
au secours!	*help!*
bien sûr	*of course*
bon voyage	*have a good journey*
bonjour	*hello, good morning*
bonne journée	*have a good day*
bonne nuit	*goodnight*
bonne soirée	*have a good evening*
bonsoir	*good evening*
de rien	*don't mention it*
Je t'/vous en prie	*It's a pleasure*
non merci	*no thank you*
pardon?	*I beg your pardon?, Pardon?*
prière de	*please (request – formal)*
le rendez-vous	*meeting, meeting place*
rendez-vous à six heures	*meet you at 6 o'clock*
s'il te plaît/s'il vous plaît	*please (informal)/please (polite)*
salut	*hi*
veuillez	*please (request – formal)*

Had a look ☐ **Nearly there** ☐ **Nailed it** ☐

Module 1 Vocabulaire

Words I should know for speaking and writing activities

La famille — *Family members*
- le beau-père — *stepfather/father-in-law*
- la belle-mère — *stepmother/mother-in-law*
- le beau-frère — *brother-in-law*
- la belle-sœur — *sister-in-law*
- le demi-frère — *half-brother/stepbrother*
- la demi-sœur — *half-sister/stepsister*
- la fille — *daughter*
- le fils — *son*
- l'enfant — *child*
- le petit-enfant — *grandchild*
- le mari — *husband*
- l'ex mari (m) — *ex-husband*
- la femme — *wife*
- l'ex femme (f) — *ex-wife*

Had a look ☐ **Nearly there** ☐ **Nailed it** ☐

Les adjectifs de personnalité — *Personality adjectives*
- Il/Elle est … — *He/She is …*
- agaçant(e) — *annoying*
- aimable — *likeable*
- amusant(e) — *amusing, funny*
- arrogant(e) — *arrogant*
- bavard(e) — *talkative, chatty*
- charmant(e) — *charming*
- drôle — *funny*
- égoïste — *selfish*
- fidèle — *loyal*
- fort(e) — *strong*

Had a look ☐ **Nearly there** ☐ **Nailed it** ☐

- généreux/-euse — *generous*
- gentil(le) — *kind*
- impatient(e) — *impatient*
- jaloux/-ouse — *jealous*
- méchant(e) — *nasty*
- paresseux/-euse — *lazy*
- poli(e) — *polite*
- sage — *well-behaved, wise*
- sensible — *sensitive*
- sérieux/-euse — *serious*
- sympa (invariable) — *nice*
- sympathique — *nice*
- têtu(e) — *stubborn, pig-headed*
- travailleur/-euse — *hard-working*
- triste — *sad*

Had a look ☐ **Nearly there** ☐ **Nailed it** ☐

Ma description physique — *My physical description*
- J'ai les cheveux … — *I have … hair*
- courts/longs/mi-longs — *short/long/mid-length*
- raides/bouclés/frisés — *straight/curly*
- noirs/bruns/châtain — *black/brown/chestnut*
- blonds/roux/gris/blancs — *blond/red/grey/white*
- J'ai les yeux … — *I have … eyes*
- bleus/verts — *blue/green*
- gris/marron — *grey/brown*
- J'ai … — *I have …*
- des boutons — *spots*
- une barbe — *a beard*
- une moustache — *a moustache*
- Je suis … — *I am …*
- petit(e)/grand(e) — *short/tall*
- de taille moyenne — *of average height*
- mince/gros(se) — *slim/fat*
- beau/belle — *beautiful*
- joli(e) — *pretty*
- moche — *ugly*
- Je porte des lunettes — *I wear glasses*

Had a look ☐ **Nearly there** ☐ **Nailed it** ☐

En ville — *In town*
- la boîte de nuit — *nightclub*
- le bowling — *bowling alley*
- le café — *café*
- le centre commercial — *shopping centre*
- le cinéma — *cinema*
- les magasins (m) — *shops*
- la patinoire — *ice rink*
- la piscine — *swimming pool*
- la plage — *beach*
- le théâtre — *theatre*
- dans — *in*
- derrière — *behind*
- devant — *in front of*
- entre — *between*
- en face de — *opposite*
- à côté de — *next to*
- près de — *near*

Had a look ☐ **Nearly there** ☐ **Nailed it** ☐

Quand? — *When?*
- aujourd'hui — *today*
- demain — *tomorrow*
- après-demain — *the day after tomorrow*

15

Module 1 Vocabulaire

ce matin	this morning
cet après-midi	this afternoon
ce soir	tonight

Had a look ☐ Nearly there ☐ Nailed it ☐

L'amitié / *Friendship*

Un(e) bon(ne) ami(e) est …	*A good friend is …*
de bonne humeur	*in a good mood*
compréhensif/-ive	*understanding*
équilibré(e)	*balanced, level-headed*
honnête	*honest*
indépendant(e)	*independent*
modeste	*modest*
patient(e)	*patient*
sûr(e) de lui/elle	*self-confident*
Un(e) bon(ne) ami(e) n'est pas …	*A good friend is not …*
de mauvaise humeur	*in a bad mood*
déprimé(e)	*depressed*
pessimiste	*pessimistic*
prétentieux/-euse	*pretentious*
vaniteux/-euse	*conceited*
Il/Elle …	*He/She …*
croit en moi	*believes in me*
dit toujours la vérité	*always tells the truth*
me fait rire	*makes me laugh*
prend soin de moi	*takes care of me*
voit le bon côté des choses	*sees the positive side of things*

Had a look ☐ Nearly there ☐ Nailed it ☐

Les traits de personnalité / *Qualities*

le sens de l'humour	*a sense of humour*
la patience	*patience*
la générosité	*generosity*
la gentillesse	*kindness*
la fidélité	*loyalty*
la modestie	*modesty*
l'honnêteté (f)	*honesty*
l'optimisme (m)	*optimism*

Had a look ☐ Nearly there ☐ Nailed it ☐

On décrit un(e) ami(e) / *Describing a friend*

Il/Elle …	*He/She …*
mesure 1,68 mètre	*is 1m 68cm tall*
semble timide	*seems shy*
porte un appareil dentaire	*has a brace*
a l'air cool	*looks cool*
a les yeux qui inspirent confiance	*has eyes which inspire (sb's) confidence*
On a les mêmes centres d'intérêt.	*We have the same interests.*

Had a look ☐ Nearly there ☐ Nailed it ☐

Les rapports de famille / *Family relationships*

se confier à	*to confide in*
se disputer avec	*to argue with*
s'entendre bien avec	*to get on well with*
se fâcher contre	*to get angry with*
s'intéresser à	*to be interested in*
s'occuper de	*to look after*
s'aimer	*to love each other*
se chamailler	*to bicker with each other*
mort(e)/décédé(e)	*dead*
divorcé(e)(s)	*divorced*
séparé(e)(s)	*separated*

Had a look ☐ Nearly there ☐ Nailed it ☐

On décrit sa famille / *Describing family members*

adorable	*adorable*
débrouillard(e)	*resourceful*
dynamique	*lively*
énergique/plein(e) d'énergie	*energetic*
extraverti(e)	*outgoing*
fragile	*fragile*
instable	*unstable*
introverti(e)	*introverted*

Had a look ☐ Nearly there ☐ Nailed it ☐

On va sortir / *Going out*

Je vais/Tu vas/On va…	*I'm going/You're going/We're going…*
aller au match	*to go to the match*
faire les magasins	*to go shopping*
faire du patin à glace/du patinage	*to go ice-skating*
manger au fast-food	*to eat in a fast-food restaurant*
aller au cinéma	*to go to the cinema*
faire du skate	*to go skateboarding*
voir un spectacle	*to see a show*
jouer à des jeux vidéo	*to play video games*
venir chez moi	*to come to my house*
Tu veux venir?	*Do you want to come?*
Tu peux venir?	*Can you come?*

Module 1 Vocabulaire

On se retrouve quand?	When will we meet?
… où?	Where …?
… à quelle heure?	At what time …?
Tu y vas avec qui?	Who are you going there with?
… comment?	How …?
D'accord.	OK.
À plus!/À plus tard!	See you later!

Had a look ☐ **Nearly there** ☐ **Nailed it** ☐

On décrit une sortie — Describing a night out

hier soir	last night
à 20 heures	at 8 p.m.
d'abord	first of all
après	afterwards
puis/ensuite	then
J'ai …/Il/Elle a …/Nous avons …	I …/He/She …/We …
visité le musée	visited the museum
vu un match/une exposition	saw a match/an exhibition
mangé dans un restaurant	ate in a restaurant
refusé de manger	refused to eat
bu un coca	drank a cola
dit «au revoir»	said 'good-bye'
embrassé	kissed

Had a look ☐ **Nearly there** ☐ **Nailed it** ☐

Je suis …/Il/Elle est …/ Nous sommes …	I …/He/She …/We …
allé(e)(s) à un pub	went to a pub
resté(e)(s) dehors sur la terrasse	stayed outside on the terrace
entré(e)(s) dans un restaurant	went into a restaurant
sorti(e)(s)	went out
parti(e)(s)	left
monté(e)(s) dans le bus	got on the bus
rentré(e)(s) à la maison	went home
tombé(e)(s) amoureux/-euse(s)	fell in love

Had a look ☐ **Nearly there** ☐ **Nailed it** ☐

Parler de son enfance — Talking about your childhood

Quand j'étais plus jeune, …	When I was younger, …
j'habitais avec (mon papa et ma maman)	I lived with (my mum and dad)
j'allais à l'école primaire	I went to primary school
j'avais (les cheveux blonds)	I had (blond hair)
j'étais (mignon(ne))	I was (cute)
je jouais (à «cache-cache»)	I played ('hide and seek')
j'aimais (les bonbons)	I liked (sweets)
je détestais (les épinards)	I hated (spinach)
je portais (un maillot du PSG)	I wore (a PSG shirt)
je rêvais d'être …	my dream was to be a …

Had a look ☐ **Nearly there** ☐ **Nailed it** ☐

Qui est-ce que tu admires? — Who do you admire?

Mon modèle s'appelle …	My role model is called …
Moi, j'admire …	Personally I admire …
Mon héros/Mon héroïne, c'est …	My hero/heroine is …
J'aimerais bien être comme lui/elle.	I would like to be like him/her.
J'admire sa créativité.	I admire his/her creativity.
Il/Elle …	He/She …
m'impressionne énormément	impresses me a lot
a travaillé très dur pour devenir …	worked very hard to become …
est devenu(e) …	became …
aide/a aidé …	helps/helped …
a/avait du courage/ de la détermination	has/had courage/ determination
est/était courageux/ -euse face à des dangers terribles	is/was brave when faced with terrible danger
lutte/a lutté pour …	fights/fought for …
a obtenu …	obtained/got …
a sauvé la vie de …	saved the life of …
C'est un enfant adopté, comme moi.	He/She is adopted, like me.

Had a look ☐ **Nearly there** ☐ **Nailed it** ☐

17

Module 1 Vocabulaire

Extra words I should know for reading and listening activities

Les descriptions	*Descriptions*	**Les verbes**	*Verbs*
laid(e)*	*ugly*	admirer	*to admire*
têtu(e)	*stubborn*	prendre soin de	*to take care of*
instable	*unstable*	se chamailler	*to argue*
débrouillard(e)	*resourceful*	porter	*to wear*
extraverti(e)	*extrovert*	dire la vérité	*to tell the truth*
introverti(e)	*introvert*	croire en quelqu'un	*to believe in someone*
agaçant(e)	*annoying*	briser en morceaux	*to break into pieces*
fidèle	*loyal*	diffuser	*to broadcast*
honnête	*honest*	envoyer	*to send*
sage	*wise*	libérer	*to free*
curieux/-euse	*curious*	voir le bon côté	*to see the good side*
déprimant(e)	*depressing*	rêver de	*to dream of*
défavorisé(e)	*underprivileged*	se fâcher contre	*to be angry with*
émouvant(e)	*touching*	captiver	*to captivate*
fascinant(e)	*fascinating*	tomber amoureux/-euse de**	*to fall in love with*
turbulent(e)	*boisterous*	se confier à quelqu'un**	*to confide in someone*

Had a look ☐ **Nearly there** ☐ **Nailed it** ☐

Les expressions idiomatiques	*Idioms*
maigre comme un clou	*as thin as a rake*
le top du top!	*the best!*

refuser de faire quelque chose** — *to refuse to do something*
trouver quelque chose … — *to find/think something is …*

Had a look ☐ **Nearly there** ☐ **Nailed it** ☐

Had a look ☐ **Nearly there** ☐ **Nailed it** ☐

Les noms	*Nouns*
le héros	*hero*
l'héroïne (f)	*heroine*
le modèle	*model, example*
la légende	*legend, caption*
les traits	*characteristics*
des reflets roux	*red highlights*
des sabots	*clogs*
la couture	*sewing*
le foulard	*(head)scarf*
à un très jeune âge	*at a very young age*

Had a look ☐ **Nearly there** ☐ **Nailed it** ☐

---

*Many adjectives are cognates, i.e. words that are the same or similar in two languages but beware of false friends too!

The masculine adjective *laid* means 'ugly' and the last letter *d* is silent so watch out for the pronunciation.

**Remember that verbs in French don't always have the same prepositions after them that verbs in English do, for example:

to fall in love with *tomber amoureux de* … (to fall in love of …)

18

Words I should know for speaking and writing activities

Le sport / Sport
Je fais … / I do/go …
du canoë-kayak / canoeing, kayaking
du footing / jogging
du hockey sur glace / ice hockey
du patinage / skating
du roller / roller skating
du vélo/cyclisme / cycling
de la boxe / boxing
de la danse / dancing
de la musculation / weightlifting
de la natation / swimming
de la planche à voile / windsurfing
de la voile / sailing
de l'escalade / climbing
de l'équitation / horse-riding
des randonnées / for walks
Je trouve ça … / I think it's …
bien/cool / good/cool
génial/super / great/super
passionnant / exciting
barbant/ennuyeux / boring
nul/stupide / rubbish/stupid

Had a look ☐ Nearly there ☐ Nailed it ☐

La musique / Music
Je joue … / I play …
du piano / the piano
du saxophone / the saxophone
du violon / the violin
de la batterie / drums
de la clarinette / the clarinet
de la flûte / the flute
de la guitare / the guitar
de la trompette / the trumpet
de l'accordéon / the accordion
Mon chanteur préféré, c'est … / My favourite singer is …
car j'aime ses paroles/ses mélodies / because I like his/her lyrics/tunes
J'aime aussi la musique de … / I also like …'s music.
Ça me donne envie de … / It makes me want to …
Ça me rend … / It makes me …
J'ai téléchargé/acheté … / I downloaded/bought …
Je n'aime pas du tout la musique de … / I don't like …'s music at all.
Je déteste … / I hate …

Had a look ☐ Nearly there ☐ Nailed it ☐

La technologie / Technology
Je fais … / I do …
beaucoup de choses / lots of things
des quiz/des recherches pour mes devoirs / quizzes/research for my homework
Je fais des achats. / I buy things/make purchases.
Je vais sur mes sites préférés/des blogs/des forums. / I go on my favourite sites/blogs/forums.
J'envoie des e-mails/mails. / I send emails.
Je joue à des jeux en ligne. / I play games online.

Had a look ☐ Nearly there ☐ Nailed it ☐

Films et télé / Films and TV
J'aime/J'adore les … / I like/love …
Je (ne) suis (pas) fan de … / I am (not) a fan of …
Je n'aime pas … / I don't like …
J'ai une passion pour les … / I am passionate about …
J'ai horreur des … / I hate/can't stand …
films de gangsters/d'action / gangster/action films
films d'aventure/d'horreur / adventure/horror films
films d'arts martiaux / martial arts films
films de science-fiction / science fiction films
Je préfère … / I prefer …
les documentaires / documentaries
les jeux télévisés / game shows
les magazines / magazine programmes
les séries / series
les actualités / current affairs programmes
les émissions de musique/de sport/jeunesse/de télé-réalité / music/sports/youth/reality TV programmes
Mon émission préférée, c'est … / My favourite programme is …
Je trouve ça … / I find it …
Je pense que c'est … / I think that it's …

Had a look ☐ Nearly there ☐ Nailed it ☐

Parler de sport / Talking about sport
Je fais de l'escrime/du footing depuis (quatre ans). / I've been doing fencing/jogging for (four years).
Je pratique le trampoline depuis (trois mois). / I've been trampolining for (three months).

Module 2 Vocabulaire

M2

Module 2 Vocabulaire

On joue au basket ensemble depuis (trois ans).	We've been playing basketball together for (three years).
J'aime beaucoup ça car c'est …	I like it a lot because it's …
élégant/facile	elegant/easy
ludique/sympa	fun/nice
rapide/beau	fast/pleasant
C'est un sport qui est bon pour …	It's a sport that is good for …
le corps/le cœur	the body/the heart
le mental/la concentration	the mind/concentration
… et qui demande …	… and which requires …
une excellente forme physique	excellent physical condition
une bonne coordination	good coordination
de l'endurance	endurance
de bons réflexes	good reflexes
Ça m'aide à décompresser.	It helps me to relax.
Ça me fait du bien.	It does me good.
Je préfère les sports individuels.	I prefer individual sports.
Je respire.	I breathe.
Je me fixe des objectifs.	I set goals for myself.
J'oublie mes soucis.	I forget my worries.

Had a look ☐ **Nearly there** ☐ **Nailed it** ☐

Ma vie d'internaute / My life online

Je suis passionné(e) de …	I am passionate about/a huge fan of …
photographie/cinéma/musique	photography/cinema/music
Il y a (deux mois), j'ai créé …	(Two months) ago, I created …
une page Facebook	a Facebook page
une chaîne YouTube	a YouTube channel
une station de radio	a radio station
un blog	a blog
Ça (ne) marche (pas) très bien.	It's (not) working very well.
J'ai beaucoup d'abonnés et de mentions «J'aime».	I have lots of subscribers and likes.
Je vais travailler avec mon ami/ma sœur/prof …	I'm going to work with my friend/sister/teacher …
car il/elle est plus/moins … que moi	because he/she is more/less … than me
arrogant(e)/créatif/-ve	arrogant/creative
modeste/patient(e)	modest/patient
optimiste/organisé(e)	optimistic/organised
sérieux/-euse/technophobe	serious/technophobic
Nous allons créer …	We're going to create …

Had a look ☐ **Nearly there** ☐ **Nailed it** ☐

La lecture / Books and reading

Quand j'avais X ans, je lisais …	When I was X years old, I read …
J'aimais …	I liked …
Avant, avec mes enfants, on lisait …	In the past, I read … with my children.
des histoires/des romans	stories/novels
des livres illustrés/classiques	illustrated books/classics
des livres pour enfants/des journaux	children's books/newspapers
Maintenant, je lis …	Now I read …
sur ma tablette/mon ordi	on my tablet/my computer

Had a look ☐ **Nearly there** ☐ **Nailed it** ☐

Sur Internet / On the internet

Maintenant/Aujourd'hui, les jeunes …	Now/Today, young people …
lisent des blogs/des textos/des tweets	read blogs/texts/tweets
passent tout leur temps sur leur portable	spend all their time on their mobile
Je trouve ça génial.	I find that great.
Je trouve que c'est bien/mieux/un peu dommage.	I find that it's good/better/a bit of a shame.
À mon avis, Internet a tué les joies de la lecture.	In my opinion, the internet has killed the joy of reading.

Had a look ☐ **Nearly there** ☐ **Nailed it** ☐

Mes émissions préférées / My favourite TV programmes

Mon émission de télé préférée, c'est …	My favourite TV programme is …
C'est (un docu-réalité) qui parle de …	It's (a reality documentary) about …
Je le/la regarde …	I watch it …
toutes les semaines	every week
tous les jours/mois	every day/month
Je le/la trouve formidable/super/génial(e).	I find it amazing/fantastic/great.
Je ne le/la rate/manque jamais.	I never miss it.
Je ne le/la regarde jamais.	I never watch it.
Je le/la trouve débile/vulgaire.	I find it idiotic/crude.
J'adore les animateurs/animatrices.	I love the presenters.
Les acteurs sont excellents/ne sont pas crédibles.	The actors are excellent/not believable.
Le scénario n'a aucun rapport avec la réalité.	The script bears no relation to reality.

Module 2 Vocabulaire

Je le/la regarde en version originale.	I watch it in the original language.	Il/Elle est extrêmement modeste/sincère/humble.	He/she is extremely modest/sincere/humble.
Avant, je regardais/nous regardions …	Before, I/we used to watch …	J'ai vu le film … il y a un moment et depuis, je suis fan.	I saw the … film some time ago and since then, I've been a fan.
Maintenant, j'ai tendance à regarder …	Now, I tend to watch …	Apparemment, quand il/elle était jeune …	Apparently, when he/she was young …
en direct sur la TNT	live on terrestrial TV	X compte parmi les acteurs les plus connus et les plus appréciés au monde.	X is one of the best-known and best-regarded actors in the world.
en replay/streaming	recorded/streamed		

Had a look ☐ **Nearly there** ☐ **Nailed it** ☐

Le cinéma	**Cinema**
Je suis passionné(e) de cinéma.	I'm passionate/mad about cinema.
J'adore …	I love …
J'admire …	I admire …
Je suis fan de … depuis	I'm a fan of … since
Il est le plus …	He is the most …
Elle est la plus …	She is the most …
beau/belle	good-looking, beautiful
intelligent(e)	intelligent
talentueux/-euse	talented
élégant(e)	elegant
doué(e)	gifted, talented
célèbre	famous
chic	chic
Chez lui/elle, il y a très peu …	With him/her, there is very little …
de prétention	pretentiousness
de vanité	vanity
d'arrogance	arrogance

J'adore ses films et je les recommande. — I love his/her films and I recommend them.
Je vais voir son prochain film très bientôt. — I'm going to see his/her next film very soon.

Had a look ☐ **Nearly there** ☐ **Nailed it** ☐

Had a look ☐ **Nearly there** ☐ **Nailed it** ☐

Module 2 Vocabulaire

Extra words I should know for reading and listening activities

Les descriptions / *Descriptions*

impatient(e)	*impatient*
charismatique	*charismatic*
arrogant(e)	*arrogant*
modeste	*modest*
créatif/-ve	*creative*
ludique	*fun*
motivant(e)	*motivating*
fédérateur/-rice	*unifying*
urbain(e)	*urban*
collectif/-ve	*collective*

Had a look ☐ **Nearly there** ☐ **Nailed it** ☐

Les nouvelles technologies / *New technologies*

les mentions (f)	*likes*
les abonné(e)s	*subscribers*
l'ambiance (f)	*atmosphere*
l'ordinateur/ordi (m)	*computer*
la chanson	*song*
le/la chanteur/-euse	*singer*
le portable	*mobile phone*
les blogs (m)*	*blogs*
les forums (m)*	*forums*
les réseaux sociaux (m)	*social networks*
les jeux en ligne (m)	*online games*
l'écran (m)	*screen*
la tablette*	*tablet*
la toile	*the web*
les textos (m)*	*texts*

Had a look ☐ **Nearly there** ☐ **Nailed it** ☐

Les idées / *Concepts*

la généalogie	*genealogy*
la souplesse	*flexibility*
le corps	*body*
le mental	*mind*
l'endurance (f)	*endurance, stamina*
la persévérance	*perseverance*
le projet	*plan*
les joies (f)	*joys*
la perte de temps	*waste of time*

Had a look ☐ **Nearly there** ☐ **Nailed it** ☐

Les expressions / *Expressions*

Ça m'énerve!**	*That annoys me!*
Ça m'amuse!**	*That makes me laugh!*
Ça marche bien!**	*That works well!*
Ça me passionne!**	*That fascinates me!*
Je décompresse!	*I chill out!*
Je suis passionné(e) de …	*I'm a keen …*
Je prends plaisir à …	*I enjoy …*

Had a look ☐ **Nearly there** ☐ **Nailed it** ☐

 Lots of new technology-related words are the same in French as in English, for example, des blogs.

**French people use Ça over and over in everyday language – try to learn as many expressions as you can with it in to increase your fluency!

Module 3 Vocabulaire

Words I should know for speaking and writing activities

Repas et nourriture — Meals and food

Je bois/mange/prends …	I drink/eat/have …
du café/lait/jus d'orange	coffee/milk/orange juice
du pain grillé/beurre	toast/butter
du yaourt/miel	yogurt/honey
du poulet/jambon/poisson	chicken/ham/fish
du saucisson/fromage	sausage/cheese
du pain/riz	bread/rice
du chou-fleur/raisin	cauliflower/grapes
de la confiture/glace	jam/ice cream
de la soupe/viande	soup/meat
de la mousse au chocolat/tarte au citron	chocolate mousse/lemon tart
de l'eau (minérale) (f)	(mineral) water
des fruits (m)/bananes (f)	fruit/bananas
des fraises (f)/pêches (f)	strawberries/peaches
des pommes (f)/poires (f)	apples/pears
des légumes (m)/petits pois (m)	vegetables/peas
des champignons (m)/haricots verts (m)	mushrooms/green beans
des carottes (f)/pommes de terre (f)	carrots/potatoes
des céréales (f)/pâtes (f)	cereal/pasta
des crudités (f)/œufs (m)	crudités/eggs

Had a look ☐ **Nearly there** ☐ **Nailed it** ☐

Je ne mange pas de viande.	I don't eat meat.
Je suis végétarien(ne).	I'm vegetarian.
un paquet de …	a packet of …
un kilo de …	a kilo of …
une bouteille de …	a bottle of …
un pot de …	a jar/pot of …
cinq cents grammes de …	500 grams of …
quatre tranches de …	four slices of …
un morceau de …	a piece of …
un litre de …	a litre of …
une boîte de …	a tin/can of …
Il faut aller …	You need to go …
à la boucherie	to the butcher's
à la boulangerie	to the baker's
à la charcuterie	to the deli/pork butcher's
à la pâtisserie	to the cake shop
à l'épicerie (f)	to the grocer's
au marché	to the market

Had a look ☐ **Nearly there** ☐ **Nailed it** ☐

Les vêtements — Clothes

D'habitude, je porte …	Usually I wear …
Je vais mettre …	I'm going to put on …
J'ai mis …	I put on …
un blouson	a jacket
un chapeau	a hat
un collant	tights
un costume	a suit
un jean moulant	skinny jeans
un manteau	a coat
un pantalon	trousers
un polo	a polo shirt
un pull	a sweater

Had a look ☐ **Nearly there** ☐ **Nailed it** ☐

un sac à main	a handbag
un short	shorts
un sweat à capuche	a hoody
un tee-shirt	a T-shirt
une casquette	a cap
une ceinture	a belt
une chemise	a shirt
une cravate	a tie
une écharpe	a scarf
une mini-jupe	a mini-skirt
une robe	a dress
une veste	a jacket
des baskets (f)	trainers
des bottes (f)	boots
des chaussettes (f)	socks
des chaussures (f)	shoes
des gants (m)	gloves
des lunettes de soleil (f)	sunglasses

Had a look ☐ **Nearly there** ☐ **Nailed it** ☐

blanc(he)(s)	white
bleu(e)(s)	blue
gris(e)(s)	grey
jaune(s)	yellow
kaki	khaki
marron	brown
mauve(s)	purple
noir(e)(s)	black
orange	orange
rose(s)	pink
rouge(s)	red
vert(e)(s)	green
en coton/cuir/laine/soie	(made of) cotton/leather/wool/silk

Module 3 Vocabulaire

rayé(e)	striped
à carreaux	checked
de marque	designer
habillé(e)	smart
de couleur vive	brightly-coloured
multicolore	multi-coloured
foncé(e)	dark

Had a look ☐ Nearly there ☐ Nailed it ☐

La vie quotidienne — *Daily life*

J'ai cours …	I have lessons …
tous les jours sauf …	every day except …
(cinq) jours par semaine	(five) days a week
Je vais au lycée …	I go to school …
en bus/en scooter/en voiture/à pied	by bus/by moped/by car/on foot
Les jours d'école, …	On school days …
je dois me lever tôt	I have to get up early
je prends mon petit-déjeuner	I have my breakfast
je quitte la maison	I leave the house
Le dimanche, …	On Sundays …
je peux rester au lit/faire la grasse matinée	I can stay in bed/have a lie-in
Le soir, …	In the evening …
je dois faire mes devoirs	I have to do my homework
je mange avec ma famille	I eat with my family
je regarde un peu la télé	I watch a bit of TV
Le mercredi/samedi après-midi, …	On Wednesday/Saturday afternoon …
je peux me détendre un peu	I can relax a bit
je reste à la maison/chez moi	I stay at home
Le week-end, …	At the weekend …
je sors avec mes copains	I go out with friends
je dois aider ma mère/mon père	I have to help my mum/dad
je vais au cinéma/au bowling	I go to the cinema/bowling

Had a look ☐ Nearly there ☐ Nailed it ☐

Les repas de fêtes — *Food for special occasions*

Ma fête préférée est …	My favourite festival is …
Noël/le 5 novembre/Hanoukka/Aïd el-Fitr/Diwali	Christmas/5 November/Hanukkah/Eid al-Fitr/Diwali
parce que j'adore …	because I love …
D'habitude, je le/la fête …	I usually celebrate it …
en famille/chez nous	with my family/at home
chez mon/ma/mes …/avec …	at my …'s house/with …
On fait/décore/se souhaite …	We do/decorate/wish each other …
D'abord, on mange/boit … suivi(e) par …	First we eat/drink …, followed by …
de la dinde	turkey
une bûche de Noël	Yule log
Dedans, il y a …	Inside, there is …
C'est mon/ma/mes … qui prépare(nt) …	My … prepare(s) …
Après le repas, on …	After the meal we …
s'offre (des cadeaux)	give each other (presents)
admire (le sapin de Noël)	admire the (Christmas tree)
chante/danse	sing/dance

Had a look ☐ Nearly there ☐ Nailed it ☐

Les repas à la maison — *Meals at home*

Du lundi au vendredi, je prends	From Monday to Friday I have
le petit-déjeuner à … heures.	breakfast at …
Le week-end, je prends mon petit-déjeuner plus tard.	At the weekend I have my breakfast later.
Je grignote après l'école.	I have a snack after school.
Je ne grignote jamais en dehors des repas.	I never snack between meals.
Je regarde la télé en mangeant le soir.	I watch TV while eating in the evening.
Dans ma famille, on ne regarde pas la télé en mangeant.	In our family, we don't watch TV while eating.
On dîne en famille tous les jours.	We have dinner as a family every day.

Had a look ☐ Nearly there ☐ Nailed it ☐

Félicitations! — *Congratulations!*

Je suis né(e) en …	I was born in …
Je viens de fêter …	I have just celebrated …
Il y a (trois) mois, j'ai fêté …	(Three) months ago I celebrated …
C'était mon quatorzième/quinzième anniversaire.	It was my fourteenth/fifteenth birthday.
J'ai reçu beaucoup de …	I received lots of …
J'ai invité … à un barbecue/une fête chez moi.	I invited … to a barbecue/party at my house.

Module 3 Vocabulaire

Je suis allé(e) au mariage (de mon cousin) à la mairie avec toute ma famille.	*I went to (my cousin's) wedding at the town hall with all my family.*	Mardi Gras	*Shrove Tuesday*
		1er Avril	*April Fool's Day*
		Pâques	*Easter*
On a mangé/écouté/ dansé/joué/fait/vu …	*We ate/listened to/danced/ played/did/saw …*	la fête du Travail	*May Day/Labour Day*
		la fête des Mères	*Mother's Day*
C'était une excellente soirée!	*It was an excellent evening!*	la fête de la Musique	*music festival in France on 21 June*
Pour fêter mon prochain anniversaire, je vais …	*To celebrate my next birthday, I'm going to …*	la fête nationale	*Bastille Day, 14 July*
		la Nuit Blanche	*first Saturday of October, when many museums and art galleries stay open all night*

Had a look ☐ **Nearly there** ☐ **Nailed it** ☐

Les fêtes en France — *Festivals in France*

	la Toussaint	*All Saints' Day*
le jour férié	*public holiday*
le jour de l'An	*New Year's Day*
la fête des Rois/ l'Épiphanie (f)	*Twelfth Night/Epiphany*
la Chandeleur	*Candlemas*
la Saint-Valentin	*St Valentine's Day*

la Toussaint	*All Saints' Day*
le jour de Noël	*Christmas Day*
la Saint-Sylvestre	*New Year's Eve*

Had a look ☐ **Nearly there** ☐ **Nailed it** ☐

Module 3 Vocabulaire

Extra words I should know for reading and listening activities

La nourriture	*Food*
le chou-fleur	*cauliflower*
la bûche de Noël	*yule log*
le réveillon	*New Year's Eve meal*
la galette des rois	*special cake made to be eaten at Epiphany*
les verrines (f)	*verrines/tumblers/bite-size desserts*
la fève	*lucky charm put into the 'galette des rois'*
les épinards (m)	*spinach*
le saumon	*salmon*
la salade composée	*mixed salad*
le croquembouche	*profiterole-based dessert, built into a tower, quite often eaten as a cake at weddings*

Had a look ☐ Nearly there ☐ Nailed it ☐

Les jours de fête	*Celebrations*
la fête	*festivities, festival*
les noces d'argent (f)	*silver wedding anniversary*
la bague	*ring*
la mairie	*town hall*
le témoin	*witness*
le feu d'artifice	*fireworks*
le déguisement	*costume*
la reine	*queen*
les chars fleuris (m)	*flower-decked floats*
la Toussaint	*All Souls' Day (1 November)*
la Nuit Blanche	*an all-night or night-time arts festival, held every year in France on the first Saturday in October, where all museums, private and public art galleries and other cultural institutions are open free to the public*
le pays natal	*country of birth*

Had a look ☐ Nearly there ☐ Nailed it ☐

Décrire les fêtes	*Describing celebrations*
apprécié(e)	*appreciated*
partagé(e)	*shared*
attaché(e)	*attached*
élaboré(e)	*developed*
multicolore	*multicoloured*
prêt(e)	*ready*
loué(e)	*hired/rented*
gratuit(e)	*free*
alimentaire	*foodstuff*
pareil(le)	*same*
fier/-ière de	*proud of*
en soie*	*made of silk*
en laine*	*made of wool*
de marque*	*branded*
de couleur vive*	*brightly coloured*

Had a look ☐ Nearly there ☐ Nailed it ☐

Verbes	*Verbs*
se pacser	*to have a civil partnership*
grignoter	*to snack*
fêter	*to celebrate*
cacher	*to hide*
faire la grasse matinée	*to lie in*
être allergique à …	*to be allergic to …*
avoir horreur de …	*to hate …*
avoir lieu**	*to take place*
ajouter	*to add*
en mangeant …	*whilst eating …*

Had a look ☐ Nearly there ☐ Nailed it ☐

Les expressions idiomatiques	*Idioms*
Ne t'en fais pas!	*Don't worry about it!*
Et voilà!	*There you go!*

Had a look ☐ Nearly there ☐ Nailed it ☐

---

*Use *en* to refer to what something is made of.

Elle porte une robe en soie et lui un costume en laine.

Use the preposition *de* to indicate what type of item it is and to convey more description.

Benjamin aime les vêtements de marque et de couleur vive.

**The verb *avoir* is used for many idiomatic expressions that will help you sound more fluent in your writing and your speaking.

Examples: *avoir lieu* to take place; *en avoir marre* to have had enough.

La fête a lieu le 23 septembre. The festival takes place on the 23rd of September.

Le travail, c'est dur! J'en ai marre! Working is hard! I've had enough!

Module 4 Vocabulaire

Words I should know for speaking and writing activities

Où j'habite / *Where I live*
J'habite … / *I live …*
Ma famille et moi habitons … / *My family and I live …*
On habite … / *We live …*
dans une ville historique/touristique / *in an historic/touristy town*
dans un petit village / *in a small village*
au bord de la mer / *at the seaside*
au centre-ville / *in the town centre*
à la campagne/montagne / *in the countryside/mountains*
en ville / *in town*
en Angleterre/Écosse/Irlande (du Nord)/Afrique / *in England/Scotland/(Northern) Ireland/Africa*
au Maroc/pays de Galles / *in Morocco/Wales*
aux Antilles / *in the West Indies*
à Paris/Birmingham / *in Paris/Birmingham*

Had a look ☐ **Nearly there** ☐ **Nailed it** ☐

dans le nord-est du/de la/de l'/des … / *in the north-east of …*
le nord/le nord-est / *north/north-east*
l'est/le sud-est / *east/south-east*
le sud/le sud-ouest / *south/south-west*
l'ouest/le nord-ouest / *west/north-west*
Dans ma région, il y a … / *In my region there is/are …*
des vignobles/stations de ski / *vineyards/ski resorts*
des collines/forêts / *hills/forests*
des fermes/champs / *farms/fields*
un port de pêche / *a fishing port*
un lac / *a lake*
C'est super parce qu'en hiver/en été, on peut (faire du ski/de l'escalade). / *It's great because in winter/summer, you can (go skiing/climbing).*

Had a look ☐ **Nearly there** ☐ **Nailed it** ☐

Le temps / *Weather*
Il fait beau/mauvais. / *The weather's good/bad.*
Il fait chaud/froid. / *It's hot/cold.*
Il y a du soleil. / *It's sunny.*
Il y a du brouillard/du vent. / *It's foggy/windy.*
Il y a un orage. / *There's a storm.*
Il pleut/neige/gèle. / *It's raining/snowing/icy.*
Ici, le climat est humide/sec. / *Here, the climate is wet/dry.*
Il peut faire très chaud/froid/doux. / *It can be very hot/cold/mild.*
Il ne fait pas trop chaud/froid … / *It's not too hot/cold …*

au printemps / *in spring*
en été/automne/hiver / *in summer/autumn/winter*

Had a look ☐ **Nearly there** ☐ **Nailed it** ☐

Les transports / *Transport*
Je vais/peux aller au collège … / *I go/can go to school …*
à pied/vélo / *on foot/by bike*
en train/métro/car/voiture/bus / *by train/underground/coach/car/bus*
Les transports en commun sont bons. / *The public transport is good.*

Had a look ☐ **Nearly there** ☐ **Nailed it** ☐

En ville / *In town*
Il y a … / *There is/are …*
un château / *a castle*
un centre de loisirs / *a leisure centre*
un marché / *a market*
un musée / *a museum*
un parc/jardin public / *a (public) park*
un stade / *a stadium*
un supermarché / *a supermarket*
un théâtre / *a theatre*
une bibliothèque / *a library*
une cathédrale / *a cathedral*
une église / *a church*
une gare (SNCF) / *a (train) station*
une mairie / *a town hall*
une mosquée / *a mosque*
une pharmacie / *a chemist*
une poste (un bureau de poste) / *a post office*
des hôtels / *hotels*

Had a look ☐ **Nearly there** ☐ **Nailed it** ☐

beaucoup de magasins / *lots of shops*
Il n'y a pas de … / *There isn't a/aren't any …*
Est-ce qu'il y a un/une/des … près d'ici/par ici? / *Is/Are there a/some … near here?*
Va/Allez tout droit. / *Go straight on.*
Tourne/Tournez à droite/gauche. / *Turn right/left.*
Prends/Prenez la première/deuxième droite/gauche. / *Take the first/second road on the right/left.*
Continue/Continuez jusqu'au carrefour/jusqu'aux feux / *Continue as far as the crossroads/traffic lights*
Traverse/Traversez la place/le pont. / *Cross the square/bridge.*
Descends/Descendez la rue. / *Go down the road.*
C'est … / *It's …*

27

Module 4 Vocabulaire

(assez) loin/tout près	(quite) a long way/very close	Ça ne me dit rien.	I don't fancy that.
sur ta/votre droite/gauche	on your right/left	Je n'en ai pas tellement envie.	I don't really feel like it.
au coin	on the corner	Ça a l'air nul!	That sounds rubbish!
en face (du/de la/de l'/des)	opposite		
à côté (du/de la/de l'/des)	next to		

Had a look ☐   Nearly there ☐   Nailed it ☐

Had a look ☐   Nearly there ☐   Nailed it ☐

Ma région / My region

Ma région/Une région que je connais bien, c'est …	My region/A region that I know well is …
C'est dans le (nord/sud) de …	It's in the (north/south) of …
près de la Manche/la frontière allemande/espagnole	near the English Channel/the German/Spanish border
J'y habite depuis …/J'y vais …	I have lived there since …/I have been going there …
Le paysage/La côte est vraiment magnifique/impressionnant(e).	The landscape/coast is really wonderful/impressive.
On peut y faire/visiter/voir …	You can do/visit/see … there.
La région est connue pour …	The region is known for …
Une personne célèbre qui est née en …, c'est …	A famous person who was born in … is …

Had a look ☐   Nearly there ☐   Nailed it ☐

Les renseignements / Information

Qu'est-ce qu'on va faire à …?	What are we going to do in …?
Je veux absolument (faire une promenade en bateau).	I definitely want to (go on a boat trip).
J'ai envie de (louer un bateau).	I feel like (hiring a boat).
Ça m'intéresse de voir …	I'm interested in seeing …
Je tiens à (visiter l'aquarium).	I'm keen on (visiting the aquarium).
Je voudrais aller au/à la/à l'/aux …	I would like to go to …
J'aimerais bien monter à la/au …	I would like to go up …
Je ne veux pas rater/manquer (l'exposition sur) …	I don't want to miss (the exhibition on) …
Bonne idée. Pourquoi pas?	Good idea. Why not?
Je veux bien faire ça aussi.	I want to do that too.
D'accord. Ça m'est égal.	OK. I don't mind.

Ville de rêve ou ville de cauchemar? / Dream town or nightmare town?

J'habite à …	I live in …
C'est un petit village/une grande ville dans …	It's a small village/big town in …
J'habite dans la banlieue/un quartier de …	I live in the suburbs/a district of …
Ce qui me plaît ici, c'est qu'il y a …	What I like is that …
En été/hiver, on peut …	In summer/winter, you can …
Le problème, c'est que qu' …	The problem is that …
il n'y a pas assez de (magasins/espaces verts)	there is/are not enough (shops/green spaces)
il n'y a plus de (cinéma)	there is/are no longer (a cinema)
il n'y a ni (parc) ni (aire de jeux)	there is neither (a park) nor (a play area)
il n'y a aucun (bowling)	there isn't a (single) (bowling alley)
il n'y a aucune (zone piétonne)	there isn't a (single) (pedestrian area)
il n'y a qu'un seul (magasin)	there is only one (shop)
il n'y a qu'une seule (rue)	there is just one (street)
il n'y a rien pour les jeunes	there is nothing for young people
il n'y a pas grand-chose à faire	there's not a lot to do

Had a look ☐   Nearly there ☐   Nailed it ☐

Il y a …	There is/are …
beaucoup de monde/de voitures	lots of people/cars
trop de circulation/de gens	too much traffic/too many people
tellement de bruit/de gens au chômage	so much noise/so many people out of work
peu de travail/de transports en commun/commerces	not much work/public transport/not many businesses
toujours des déchets par terre	always litter on the ground
plusieurs boîtes de nuit/cafés/restaurants	several nightclubs/cafés/restaurants
Le bowling a fermé.	The bowling alley has closed down.

Module 4 Vocabulaire

C'est sale/(trop) tranquille/très animé.	It's dirty/(too) quiet/very lively.	beau/chaud/froid/frais	fine/hot/cold/cool
Ce n'est jamais tranquille.	It's never quiet.	Le temps sera … brumeux/ensoleillé nuageux/orageux variable	The weather will be … misty/sunny cloudy/stormy changeable
Je trouve ça triste/ déprimant/affreux/nul/ désagréable.	I find that sad/ depressing/awful/ rubbish/unpleasant.	Le ciel sera bleu/gris/ couvert.	The sky will be blue/grey/ overcast.
En général, je (ne) suis (pas) content(e) de mon village/quartier/ ma ville.	In general, I am (not) happy with my village/ district/town.	Les températures seront en baisse/en hausse.	The temperatures will be going down/going up.

Had a look ☐ Nearly there ☐ Nailed it ☐

Had a look ☐ Nearly there ☐ Nailed it ☐

Les projets / Plans

Qu'est-ce qu'on fera? — What shall we do?
On ira pique-niquer dans le parc. — We'll have a picnic in the park.
Ce sera génial! — That will be great!
Je resterai à la maison. — I will stay at home.
Je regarderai un film. — I will watch a film.
Je jouerai à des jeux vidéo/au football. — I will play video games/football.
On ne fera pas de barbecue. — We won't have a barbecue.
On mangera dans un restaurant. — We will eat in a restaurant.

Had a look ☐ Nearly there ☐ Nailed it ☐

Quel temps fera-t-il? / What will the weather be like?

Il y aura … — There will be …
du vent — wind
du soleil — sun
du tonnerre — thunder
de la grêle — hail
de la pluie — rain
des averses — showers
des éclairs — lightning
des éclaircies — sunny intervals
Il fera … — It will be …

En pleine action! / Taking action

J'ai/Nous avons … — I/We have …
collecté de l'argent — collected money
vendu nos vieux jeux et jouets — sold our old games and toys
lavé des voitures — washed cars
acheté (de la peinture) — bought (paint)
planté des arbres — planted trees
lancé une pétition en ligne — launched an online petition
obtenu presque 2 000 signatures — obtained nearly 2,000 signatures
écrit un article dans le journal local — written an article in the local newspaper

Had a look ☐ Nearly there ☐ Nailed it ☐

Le week-end prochain, nous irons là-bas pour … — Next weekend, we will go there to …
ramasser les déchets — pick up litter
nettoyer la salle — clean the room
repeindre les murs — repaint the walls
La semaine prochaine, on finira d'installer/de construire … — Next week, we will finish installing/building …
un passage piéton — a pedestrian crossing
un panneau — a sign
une aire de jeux — a play area

Had a look ☐ Nearly there ☐ Nailed it ☐

Module 4 Vocabulaire

Extra words I should know for reading and listening activities

La géographie	Geography
la principauté	principality
le paysage	landscape, scenery
les Bretons (m)*	people from Brittany
le panorama	panorama
le quartier	area
la province	province
le milieu	environment
les gorges (f)	gorges
les collines (f)	hills

Had a look ☐ Nearly there ☐ Nailed it ☐

Les sports extrêmes / Extreme sports
le canyoning	canyoning
le saut à l'élastique	bungee jumping

Had a look ☐ Nearly there ☐ Nailed it ☐

Le climat / Climate
le changement climatique	climate change
le climat	climate
le mistral	cold, northerly wind
la vague de chaleur	heatwave
la canicule	scorching heat, heatwave
la tempête	storm
l'ouragan (m)	hurricane
le cyclone	cyclone

Had a look ☐ Nearly there ☐ Nailed it ☐

En route! / On the road!
la limite de vitesse	speed limit
les transports en commun (m)	public transport
les déchets (m)	rubbish
la circulation	traffic
les routes (f)	roads
les distributeurs de billets (m)	cash machines
les morts (f)	deaths

Had a look ☐ Nearly there ☐ Nailed it ☐

En ville / In town
les missions de volontariat (f)	volunteering
les promenades commentées (f)	guided tours
les stations de ski (f)	ski resorts
les stations balnéaires (f)	seaside resorts

Had a look ☐ Nearly there ☐ Nailed it ☐

Les milieux / Environments
défavorisé(e)	underprivileged
déprimant(e)	depressing
majestueux/-euse	majestic
véritable	real
les parfumeries (f)	perfumeries
les vignobles (m)	vineyards
les ateliers (m) de poterie (f)	potteries

Had a look ☐ Nearly there ☐ Nailed it ☐

Les verbes / Verbs
arrêter	to stop
causer	to cause
ramasser	to collect
collecter	to collect
repeindre	to repaint
installer	to install
savoir**	to know
connaître**	to know

Had a look ☐ Nearly there ☐ Nailed it ☐

Les expressions idiomatiques / Idioms
pas tellement mon truc!	not really my thing!
ma mission à moi, c'est ...	my task is to ...
un spectacle son et lumière	a sound and light show

Had a look ☐ Nearly there ☐ Nailed it ☐

---

 *Use *les* + adjective of a region to indicate where a group of people are from.

Examples:

Les Bretons people from Brittany

Les Provençaux people from Provence

Les Lyonnais people from the Lyon region

Les Charentais people from the Charente region

 **These two verbs have the same translation but are used in different contexts:

connaître to know people, places, the existence of something and the value of something.

Je connais Lyon, c'est chouette! I know Lyon, it's great!

savoir to know how to do something, to know information you are aware of and to know of events.

Je sais nager. I know how to swim.

Module 5 Vocabulaire

Words I should know for speaking and writing activities

En vacances	*On holiday*
l'Algérie (f)	Algeria
l'Allemagne (f)	Germany
l'Angleterre (f)	England
l'Autriche (f)	Austria
la Belgique	Belgium
la Croatie	Croatia
l'Espagne (f)	Spain
les États-Unis (m)	USA
la France	France
le Japon	Japan
le Pakistan	Pakistan
les Pays-Bas (m)	Netherlands
le pays de Galles	Wales
la Pologne	Poland
la Suisse	Switzerland

Had a look ☐   Nearly there ☐   Nailed it ☐

Normalement, je passe mes vacances en/au/à l'/aux …	Normally, I spend my holidays in …
Je vais au bord de la mer/à la campagne/à la montagne.	I go to the seaside/the countryside/the mountains.
Je voyage en train/avion/ferry/voiture.	I go by train/plane/ferry/car.
Je fais du camping.	I go camping.
Je loge dans un gîte/un hôtel/chez ma tante.	I stay in a holiday cottage/a hotel/with my aunt.
J'y vais avec ma famille/mes grand-parents/mon petit frère.	I go there with my family/my grandparents/my little brother.
C'est génial/extra/assez ennuyeux.	It's great/excellent/quite boring.
Je me lève tôt.	I get up early.
On se couche tard.	We go to bed late.
Je me repose/me prépare.	I rest/get ready.
Je m'habille.	I get dressed.
Je vais à la plage.	I go to the beach.
Je me baigne dans la mer.	I bathe/swim in the sea.
Je me promène.	I go for a walk.
Je rentre à l'hôtel.	I go back to the hotel.
Je sors au restaurant.	I go out to a restaurant.
On peut …	You can …
faire une visite de Paris	visit Paris
faire de l'escalade	go climbing
visiter les musées/monuments	visit museums/monuments
aller à la pêche/à la plage	go fishing/to the beach
jouer à la pétanque	play petanque, boules

Had a look ☐   Nearly there ☐   Nailed it ☐

Les vacances passées et futures	*Holidays past and future*
Tous les ans/Normalement/Tous les étés, …	Every year/Normally/Every summer, …
j'achète/je fais/je vais …	I buy/do/go …
Hier/L'année dernière/Le week-end dernier, …	Yesterday/Last year/Last weekend, …
j'ai vu/visité/acheté …	I saw/visited/bought …
je suis allé(e) à …	I went to …
L'année prochaine/Le week-end prochain/Demain, …	Next year/Next weekend/Tomorrow, …
je vais faire/prendre/aller/visiter …	I'm going to do/take/go/visit …

Had a look ☐   Nearly there ☐   Nailed it ☐

Des vacances de rêve	*Dream holidays*
Je logerais …	I would stay …
dans un gîte à la campagne	in a holiday cottage in the countryside
dans un hôtel 4 étoiles	in a 4-star hotel
dans une auberge de jeunesse	in a youth hostel
dans une caravane	in a caravan
dans une chambre d'hôtes	in a bed and breakfast
dans une tente, sur une île déserte	in a tent on a desert island
sur un bateau	on a boat
Je voyagerais …	I would travel …
avec mes copains/copines	with my friends
avec ma famille	with my family
avec mes parents	with my parents
avec mes grands-parents	with my grandparents
avec mon lycée	with my school
avec une organisation	with an organisation
seul(e)	alone

Had a look ☐   Nearly there ☐   Nailed it ☐

Je regarderais le coucher du soleil.	I would watch the sunset.
Je nagerais avec les poissons tropicaux.	I would swim with tropical fish.
Je ferais des randonnées.	I would go hiking.
Je ferais du canoë-kayak.	I would go canoeing.
Je me reposerais.	I would rest.
Je m'amuserais avec mes copains/copines.	I would have fun with my friends.
Je mangerais bien.	I would eat well.

M5

Module 5 Vocabulaire

Il y aurait …	There would be …
un café qui serait ouvert toute la nuit	a café which would be open all night
une salle de jeux	a games room
des feux d'artifice tous les soirs	fireworks every night
des spectacles son et lumière	sound and light shows
des visites guidées	guided tours
Il n'y aurait aucun bruit!	There would be no noise!
Il n'y aurait pas beaucoup d'adultes!	There wouldn't be many adults!
Ce serait …	It would be …
formidable	tremendous
luxueux	luxury
merveilleux	wonderful
passionnant	exciting
pittoresque	picturesque
reposant	restful
tranquille	quiet

Had a look ☐ Nearly there ☐ Nailed it ☐

À l'hôtel / At the hotel

Nous avons passé X jours dans cet hôtel/chambre d'hôte.	We spent X days at this hotel/bed and breakfast
Ça s'est très bien passé.	It all went very well.
C'était charmant/propre/bien situé.	It was charming/clean/well located.
très pratique/pas cher/super	very handy/not expensive/super
Le service était impeccable.	The service was impeccable.
Le Wi-Fi fonctionnait très bien.	The Wi-Fi worked very well.
Le petit-déjeuner était offert.	Breakfast was included.
Il y avait …	There was …
un parking tout près	parking nearby
un micro-onde/la climatisation dans la chambre	a microwave/air-conditioning in the room
Il y avait un très bon rapport qualité-prix.	It was very good value for money.
Nous y avons passé un super séjour.	We had a super stay there.

Had a look ☐ Nearly there ☐ Nailed it ☐

Je voudrais une chambre …	I would like a room …
pour une personne	for one person
pour deux personnes	for two people
avec un lit simple	with a single bed
avec un grand lit	with a double bed
avec une salle de bains	with a bathroom
avec une douche	with a shower
avec une vue sur la mer	with a sea view
Votre chambre est …	Your room is …
au rez-de-chaussée	on the ground floor
au premier/deuxième étage	on the first/second floor

Had a look ☐ Nearly there ☐ Nailed it ☐

Au restaurant / At the restaurant

Je préférerais une table …	I would prefer a table …
en terrasse/à l'intérieur	on the terrace/inside
Je vais prendre …	I will have/take …
le plat du jour/le menu à 30 euros	the dish of the day/the 30 euros set menu
(la soupe à la tomate) en entrée	(the tomato soup) for a starter
(le filet de loup de mer) comme plat principal	(the fillet of seabass) for the main course
(la mousse au chocolat) comme dessert	(the chocolate mousse) for dessert
Qu'est-ce que vous avez, comme desserts?	What desserts do you have?
On peut avoir l'addition, s'il vous plaît?	Could we have the bill, please?

Had a look ☐ Nearly there ☐ Nailed it ☐

Les prix n'étaient pas excessifs.	The prices weren't excessive.
C'était cher.	It was expensive.
L'accueil était très chaleureux.	The welcome was very warm.
Nous avons dû attendre plus de cinq minutes.	We had to wait more than five minutes.
L'ambiance était vraiment agréable.	The ambiance was really pleasant.
L'atmosphère était super bruyante.	The atmosphere was very noisy.
Le serveur/La serveuse était …	The waiter/waitress was …
très attentionné(e)/médiocre	very attentive/mediocre
À recommander!	To be recommended!
Je n'y retournerai jamais!	I will never go back there!
un couteau	a knife
une cuillère	a spoon
une fourchette	a fork
une serviette	a napkin

Had a look ☐ Nearly there ☐ Nailed it ☐

Les plats / The dishes

les entrées (f)	starters
les brochettes (f) de crevettes (f)	prawn skewers
les escargots (m)	snails
la soupe à la tomate	tomato soup
la tarte à l'oignon	onion tart
les plats principaux (m)	main dishes

Module 5 Vocabulaire

l'épaule (f) d'agneau	lamb shoulder
la cuisse de canard	duck leg
le gratin dauphinois	dauphinoise potatoes
les lasagnes (f) végétariennes	vegetarian lasagne
le loup de mer	sea bass
le poulet basquaise	Basque-style chicken
le rôti de veau	roast veal
les desserts (m)	desserts
la crème brûlée	crème brûlée
la mousse au chocolat	chocolate mousse
le roulé au chocolat	chocolate roll
le sorbet	sorbet
la tarte au citron	lemon tart
la tarte aux pommes	apple tart

Had a look ☐ Nearly there ☐ Nailed it ☐

En route!
On the road!

Si j'avais le choix, pour aller …	If I had the choice, to go …
en Inde/Russie/Chine	to India/Russia/China
au Sénégal/Vietnam/Brésil	to Senegal/Vietnam/Brazil
… je voyagerais …	… I would travel …
en car/train/avion	by coach/train/plane
à moto	by motorbike
… car c'est/ce n'est pas …	… because it is (not) …
rapide/confortable/pratique	quick/comfortable/practical
une aventure/la classe	an adventure/cool
bon pour l'environnement	good for the environment
ennuyeux	boring
fatigant	tiring
cher	expensive
un billet	a ticket
un aller simple	a single
un aller-retour	a return
en première classe	in first class
en deuxième classe	in second class
les horaires	travel time(s)
le guichet	ticket office
le quai	platform
la salle d'attente	waiting room

Had a look ☐ Nearly there ☐ Nailed it ☐

Acheter les souvenirs
Buying souvenirs

Je pense acheter (ce tagine).	I'm thinking of buying (this tagine).
Qu'est-ce que tu en penses?	What do you think of it?
Que penses-tu de (cette théière)?	What do you think of (this teapot)?
Je crois que je vais acheter (ces bijoux).	I think I'm going to buy (this jewellery).
Je veux acheter (un foulard).	I want to buy (a scarf).
Tu préfères celui-ci ou celui-là?	Do you prefer this one or that one?
Je cherche (une lanterne) pour (ma sœur).	I'm looking for (a lantern) for (my sister).
Je prends celle-ci ou celle-là.	Shall I take this one or that one?
J'ai envie de m'acheter des (gants).	I feel like buying some (gloves).
Tu trouves celles-ci comment?	What do you think of these?
Je déteste faire du shopping.	I hate going shopping.
Je suis accro au shopping.	I'm addicted to shopping.

Had a look ☐ Nearly there ☐ Nailed it ☐

C'était catastrophique!
It was catastrophic!

Avant de partir, j'avais …	Before leaving I had …
réservé mon billet d'avion	booked my plane ticket
fait ma valise/des recherches	packed my case/done some research
découvert/décidé que …	discovered/decided that …
tout préparé	prepared everything
J'étais allé(e) à l'agence de voyages.	I had gone to the travel agent's.
Mais/Pourtant …	But/However …
je me suis cassé la jambe	I broke my leg
j'ai oublié mon passeport	I forgot my passport
j'ai raté l'avion	I missed the plane
j'ai pris un coup de soleil affreux	I got terribly sunburnt
le camping-car est tombé en panne	the camper van broke down
on m'a volé mon sac à main	my handbag was stolen
Alors/Donc …	So …
j'ai dû aller au commissariat/à l'hôpital/chez le médecin	I had to go to the police station/hospital/doctor's
Quelle horreur!	How awful!
J'étais triste.	I was sad.
On était bien déçus.	We were really disappointed.

Had a look ☐ Nearly there ☐ Nailed it ☐

M5

Module 5 Vocabulaire

Extra words I should know for reading and listening activities

Les souvenirs de vacances
Holiday memories
le tagine — *Moroccan cooking pot*
la théière — *teapot*
les poissons tropicaux (m) — *tropical fish*
les créatures (f) — *creatures*

Had a look ☐ Nearly there ☐ Nailed it ☐

En vacances
On holiday!
les vacances de neige (f) — *winter holidays*
l'île déserte (f) — *desert island*
le coin de paradis — *corner of paradise*
dans un beau cadre — *in a beautiful area*
à l'intérieur — *inside*
le parc naturel — *nature/national park*
le coup de soleil — *sunburn*
les marchands (m) — *shopkeepers*
l'auberge de jeunesse (f) — *youth hostel*
la climatisation — *air-conditioning*
le pourboire — *tip*
l'hôtel 4 étoiles (m) — *4 star hotel*
la formule demi-pension — *half-board*
en montgolfière (f) — *in a hot air balloon*
le Wi-Fi — *wi-fi*

Had a look ☐ Nearly there ☐ Nailed it ☐

Les activités de vacances
Holiday activities
installer — *to put in*
emporter — *to take*
vomir — *to be sick*
être à couper le souffle — *to be breath-taking*
profiter de — *to make the most of*
se baigner — *to swim*
endormir — *to fall asleep*
rater — *to miss (bus, etc.)*
faire des recherches — *to research*
rapporter — *to bring back*
essayer — *to try*
tomber en panne — *to break down*
voler — *to steal*
hurler — *to scream*
loger — *to stay*
en regardant … — *while watching …*

Had a look ☐ Nearly there ☐ Nailed it ☐

Les expressions idiomatiques
Idioms
c'est une bonne affaire? — *is it a good deal/bargain?*
qu'est-que c'était cher! — *it was so expensive!*
chez le médecin — *at the doctor's*
à recommander! — *I would recommend it!*
le petit-déjeuner était offert!* — *breakfast was included!*

Had a look ☐ Nearly there ☐ Nailed it ☐

⭐ **Offert* really means 'offered' but it conveys the idea of 'given away with' something, so here breakfast is given away with the stay in the hotel!

Another example:

Achetez deux jeux et le troisième est offert! Buy two games and the third is free/given away!

34

Module 6 Vocabulaire

Words I should know for speaking and writing activities

Les matières — *School subjects*
le commerce — *business studies*
le dessin — *art*
les arts plastiques (m) — *fine art*
le français — *French*
le latin — *Latin*
la biologie/les sciences de la vie et de la terre — *biology*
la chimie — *chemistry*
la géographie — *geography*
la musique — *music*
la physique/les sciences physiques — *physics*
la religion — *religious studies*
la sociologie — *sociology*
la technologie — *design and technology*
l'allemand (m) — *German*
l'anglais (m) — *English*

Had a look ☐ Nearly there ☐ Nailed it ☐

l'art dramatique (m) — *drama*
l'économie (f) — *economics*
l'éducation physique et sportive/l'EPS (f) — *PE*
l'espagnol (m) — *Spanish*
l'étude des médias (f) — *media studies*
l'histoire (f) — *history*
l'histoire-géo (f) — *humanities (history and geography, studied together in France)*
l'informatique (f) — *ICT*
l'instruction civique (f) — *citizenship*
l'italien (m) — *Italian*
les arts ménagers (m) — *home technology*
les maths (f) — *maths*

Had a look ☐ Nearly there ☐ Nailed it ☐

Mon collège — *My school*
Mercredi, à 11h15, j'ai histoire-géo. — *I have humanities at 11:15 a.m. on Wednesday.*
J'ai (deux) heures de (musique) par semaine. — *I have (two) hours of (music) per week.*
Il n'y a pas de cours de ... dans mon emploi du temps. — *There are no ... lessons in my timetable.*
J'apprends (deux) langues vivantes. — *I learn (two) foreign languages.*
Mes cours finissent à (16h00) tous les jours. — *My lessons finish at (4:00 p.m.) every day.*
Je n'ai pas cours (le mercredi après-midi). — *I don't have lessons (on Wednesday afternoon).*
Ma matière préférée est ... — *My favourite subject is ...*
J'adore/j'aime/je n'aime pas/je déteste ... — *I love/like/don't like/hate ...*
Je trouve ... — *I find ...*

Had a look ☐ Nearly there ☐ Nailed it ☐

Je pense que ... est/sont ... — *I think that ... is ...*
intéressant(e)(s) — *interesting*
passionnant(e)(s) — *exciting*
ennuyeux/-euse(s) — *boring*
... parce que/qu' ... — *... because ...*
c'est facile/fascinant/difficile/utile/inutile — *it's easy/fascinating/difficult/useful/useless*
Je suis fort(e)/faible/doué(e) en ... — *I am strong/weak/gifted in ...*
Le/La prof est bon(ne)/sympa/marrant(e)/sévère/gentil(le)/impatient(e). — *The teacher is good/nice/funny/strict/kind/impatient.*
On a trop de devoirs. — *We have too much homework.*

Had a look ☐ Nearly there ☐ Nailed it ☐

Mon bahut — *My school*
Comment s'appelle ton collège? — *What's your school called?*
Mon collège s'appelle ... — *My school is called ...*
C'est quelle sorte de collège? — *What sort of school is it?*
C'est un collège mixte pour les élèves de onze à seize ans. — *It's a mixed school for pupils from 11 to 16.*
Il y a combien d'élèves? — *How many pupils are there?*
Il y a 750 élèves et quarante-cinq professeurs. — *There are 750 pupils and 45 teachers.*
Quelles sont les horaires du collège? — *What are the school hours?*
Les cours commencent à 8h30. — *Lessons start at 8:30 a.m.*
La récré est à 10h15 et dure quinze minutes. — *Break is at 10:15 a.m. and lasts 15 minutes.*
On a une heure et demie pour le déjeuner. — *We have an hour and a half for lunch.*
Les cours finissent à 16 heures. — *Lessons finish at 4:00 p.m.*

Had a look ☐ Nearly there ☐ Nailed it ☐

Il y a combien de cours par jour? — *How many lessons are there per day?*
Il y a sept cours de cinquante-cinq minutes par jour. — *There are seven lessons of 55 minutes per day.*
Le mercredi après-midi, il n'y a pas cours. — *There are no lessons on Wednesday afternoon.*
Quelles matières étudies-tu? — *What subjects do you study?*
J'étudie douze matières, dont ... — *I study 12 subjects, including ...*
Toutes mes matières sont obligatoires. — *All my subjects are compulsory.*
Quelle est ta matière préférée? — *What is your favourite subject?*

35

Module 6 Vocabulaire

Ma matière préférée, c'est (les arts ménagers) car …	My favourite subject is (home technology) because …	Le règlement scolaire	School rules
J'adore (cuisiner) car …	I love (cooking) because …	Dans cette école, il faut …	In this school, you must …
je suis doué(e) pour ça	I'm talented at that	être à l'heure	be on time
Comment sont les professeurs ?	What are your teachers like?	faire ses devoirs	do your homework
Les profs sont sympa/sévères.	The teachers are nice/strict.	porter l'uniforme scolaire	wear school uniform
Qu'est-ce que tu penses de ton collège ?	What do you think of your school?	Il ne faut pas …	You must not …
Je trouve que/qu' …	I find that …	manquer les cours	miss lessons
les journées sont trop longues	the days are too long	tricher pendant un contrôle	cheat in a test
on a trop de contrôles	we have too many tests	Il est interdit de/d' …	It is forbidden to …
les profs sont excellents	the teachers are excellent	mâcher du chewing-gum	chew gum
		utiliser son portable en classe	use your mobile in class

Had a look ☐ **Nearly there** ☐ **Nailed it** ☐

porter des bijoux/des piercings/trop de maquillage	wear jewellery/piercings/too much make-up
harceler d'autres élèves	bully other pupils
sortir de l'école pendant l'heure du déjeuner	leave school during the lunch hour

L'école chez nous, l'école chez vous
School here and with you

En Angleterre/Écosse/Irlande du Nord …	In England/Scotland/Northern Ireland …
Au pays de Galles …	In Wales …
on va à l'école de … ans à … ans	we go to school from … to … years old
l'école commence à … heures et finit à … heures	school starts at … and finishes at …
on porte un uniforme scolaire/ses propres vêtements	we wear a school uniform/our own clothes
on achète ses propres stylos et règles	we buy our own pens and rulers
on ne redouble pas	we don't repeat the year
on étudie …	we study …
Mais en France/au Canada/au Mali …	But in France/Canada/Mali …
ils vont …	they go …
l'école commence …	school starts …
ils portent …	they wear …
ils achètent …	they buy …
ils (ne) redoublent (pas)	they (don't) repeat the year
ils étudient …	they study …
Je préfère le système (anglais/français)	I prefer the (English/French) system
parce que …	because …
les horaires sont plus raisonnables	the hours are more sensible
l'uniforme scolaire est pratique/inutile	school uniform is practical/useless
l'école fournit l'équipement	school provides the equipment
le redoublement (n')est (pas) une bonne idée	repeating the year is (not) a good idea
on (n')étudie (pas) …	we/they (don't) study …

Had a look ☐ **Nearly there** ☐ **Nailed it** ☐

Had a look ☐ **Nearly there** ☐ **Nailed it** ☐

Je trouve ça …	I find that …
raisonnable	reasonable, sensible
logique	logical
juste/injuste	fair/unfair
ridicule/frustrant	ridiculous/frustrating
… parce que/car …	… because …
c'est/ce n'est pas dangereux	it's (not) dangerous
il faut protéger les jeunes	you must protect young people
on n'est pas des bébés	we're not babies
il faut respecter les autres	you must respect others
la mode n'a pas de place à l'école	fashion has no place at school
c'est/ce n'est pas important	it's (not) important
l'école, c'est pour apprendre	school is for learning
J'ai eu une heure de retenue/de colle.	I had an hour of detention.
J'ai dû copier des lignes.	I had to write lines.

Had a look ☐ **Nearly there** ☐ **Nailed it** ☐

Des conseils pour être en bonne santé
Advice for being healthy

se concentrer en classe	to concentrate in class
se coucher tôt	to go to bed early
se détendre	to relax
dormir huit heures par nuit	to sleep eight hours per night
éteindre les écrans	to turn off screens
être en bonne forme physique	to be in good physical shape

Module 6 Vocabulaire

se faire de nouveaux amis	to make new friends
faire de la méditation ou du yoga	to do meditation or yoga
faire une activité sportive	to do a sport/sporting activity
manger équilibré	to eat a balanced diet
participer à la chorale	to participate in the choir
profiter des sorties scolaires	to make the most of school trips
se reposer	to rest
respirer	to breathe
le corps	the body
l'esprit (m)	the mind
le sommeil	sleep
les matières grasses (f)	fat(s)

Had a look ☐ **Nearly there** ☐ **Nailed it** ☐

Ce que je fais — What I do

Je mange sainement.	I eat healthily.
J'essaie de manger cinq portions de fruits et de légumes par jour.	I try to eat five portions of fruit and vegetables per day.
Je suis végétarien(ne).	I'm a vegetarian.
Je mange rarement des bonbons.	I rarely eat sweets.
Je fais attention à ce que je bois.	I am careful about what I drink.
Je ne bois pas de boissons gazeuses.	I don't drink fizzy drinks.

Had a look ☐ **Nearly there** ☐ **Nailed it** ☐

Quand et comment? — When and how?

calmement	calmly
dur	hard
également	equally, also
énormément	enormously, hugely
facilement	easily
heureusement	fortunately
lentement	slowly
mieux	better
rarement	rarely
récemment	recently
régulièrement	regularly
sainement	healthily
suffisamment	enough, sufficiently
uniquement	only

Had a look ☐ **Nearly there** ☐ **Nailed it** ☐

Les vices — Vices

boire de l'alcool	to drink alcohol
se droguer	to take drugs
fumer (des cigarettes, du cannabis)	to smoke (cigarettes, cannabis)
avoir mal à la tête	to have a headache
s'isoler	to isolate yourself
souffrir de changements d'humeur	to suffer from mood swings
ivre	drunk
je suis accro à …	I'm addicted to …

Had a look ☐ **Nearly there** ☐ **Nailed it** ☐

Les opinions — Opinions

C'est un gaspillage d'argent.	It's a waste of money.
Ça coûte très cher.	It costs a lot./It's very expensive.
C'est mauvais pour la santé.	It's bad for your health.
On risque d'avoir un cancer (des poumons, du foie) ou d'autres problèmes.	You risk getting (lung, liver) cancer or other problems.
C'est dangereux.	It's dangerous.
C'est nocif.	It's harmful.
On devient facilement accro.	You become addicted easily.
On peut vite devenir dépendant.	You can quickly become dependent.
Si on fume, on sent la fumée.	If you smoke, you smell of smoke.
Ça pue.	It stinks.
Ça me donne confiance.	It gives me confidence.
Ça m'aide dans les situations sociales.	It helps me in social situations.
Je ne veux pas grossir.	I don't want to put on weight.

Had a look ☐ **Nearly there** ☐ **Nailed it** ☐

En échange — On an exchange

Pourquoi faire un échange scolaire?	Why go on a school exchange?
On se fait de nouveaux amis.	You make new friends.
On améliore ses compétences en langue.	You improve your language skills.
On habite chez une famille d'une culture différente.	You live with a family from another culture.
On visite un nouveau pays ou une nouvelle région.	You visit a new country or region.
On apprécie non seulement les différences mais aussi les similarités entre nos vies.	You appreciate not only the differences, but also the similarities between our lives.

Had a look ☐ **Nearly there** ☐ **Nailed it** ☐

M6

37

Module 6 Vocabulaire

Extra words I should know for reading and listening activities

Les personnes — *People*
le/la surveillant(e) — *supervisor*
l'internat (m) — *boarding school*
le/la collégien(ne) — *high school student (up to yr10)*
le/la correspondant(e) — *penfriend*

Had a look ☐ **Nearly there** ☐ **Nailed it** ☐

Les problèmes — *Problems*
les matières grasses (f) — *fats*
la cigarette* — *smoking*
la fumée — *smoke*
le cancer — *cancer*
le gaspillage d'argent — *waste of money*

Had a look ☐ **Nearly there** ☐ **Nailed it** ☐

La vie — *Life*
facultatif/-ve — *optional*
admis(e) — *admitted*
voisin(e) — *neighbouring*
payé par — *paid by*
nocif/-ve — *harmful*
addictif/-ve — *addictive*
réel(le) — *real*
virtuel(le) — *virtual*

Had a look ☐ **Nearly there** ☐ **Nailed it** ☐

Les activités au collège — *School activities*
les arts plastiques (m) — *fine arts*
la musculation — *body building*
l'entraînement (m) — *training*
l'instruction civique (f) — *citizenship*
le progrès — *progress*
la maternelle — *pre-school/nursery school*
le bac — *A levels*
le contrôle — *test*
la pièce de théâtre — *play*
la chorale — *choir*
la marche rapide — *power-walking*
le chant — *singing*
le sommeil — *sleep*
la scolarité — *schooling*
la mémoire — *memory*
les compétences (f) — *skills*

Had a look ☐ **Nearly there** ☐ **Nailed it** ☐

Les problèmes au collège — *School problems*
sécher les cours/manquer les cours — *to skip lessons/to truant*
en quittant … — *on leaving …*
mâcher* — *to chew*
harceler — *to bully*
tricher — *to cheat*
stresser — *to stress*
améliorer — *to improve*
manger équilibré — *to eat a balanced diet*
rester en forme — *to keep fit*

Had a look ☐ **Nearly there** ☐ **Nailed it** ☐

> ⭐ *Watch out for 'false friends' such as la cigarette and mâcher. Learn as many of them as you can so that they don't catch you out in the exam!*
>
> Another example of a false friend is the verb *redoubler*. This actually means 'to redo another school year', <u>not</u> 'to double again'.

Module 7 Vocabulaire

Words I should know for speaking and writing activities

Les professions / *Jobs*

Ma mère/Mon père est …	*My mum/dad is a(n) …*
Je voudrais être …	*I would like to be a(n) …*
acteur/-rice	*actor/actress*
agent de police	*policeman/woman*
agriculteur/-rice	*farmer*
architecte	*architect*
boucher/-ère	*butcher*
boulanger/-ère	*baker*
caissier/-ère	*cashier*
coiffeur/-euse	*hairdresser*
créateur/-rice de mode	*fashion designer*
dentiste	*dentist*
directeur/-rice	*director*
électricien(ne)	*electrician*
employé(e) de bureau	*office worker*

Had a look ☐ **Nearly there** ☐ **Nailed it** ☐

facteur/-rice	*postman/postwoman*
fonctionnaire	*civil servant*
infirmier/-ère	*nurse*
informaticien(ne)	*computer scientist*
ingénieur(e)	*engineer*
journaliste	*journalist*
maçon(ne)	*builder*
mécanicien(ne)	*mechanic*
médecin	*doctor*
professeur	*teacher*
secrétaire	*secretary*
serveur/-euse	*waiter/waitress*
soldat	*soldier*
steward/hôtesse de l'air	*flight attendant*
vendeur/-euse	*sales assistant*
vétérinaire	*vet*

Had a look ☐ **Nearly there** ☐ **Nailed it** ☐

J'adore (la campagne).	*I love (the countryside).*
Je suis passionné(e) par (la loi et la justice).	*I'm passionate about (the law and justice).*
Je suis fort(e) en (maths).	*I'm good at (maths).*
Je suis (courageux/-euse).	*I am (brave).*
(Voyager), c'est ma passion.	*(Travelling) is my passion.*
(Les avions) me fascinent.	*(Planes) fascinate me.*
Je préférerais travailler (en plein air).	*I would prefer to work (outdoors).*
Je voudrais travailler avec (des enfants).	*I would like to work with (children).*
Je voudrais/J'aimerais travailler comme …	*I would like to work as …*
Je veux être …	*I want to be …*

Had a look ☐ **Nearly there** ☐ **Nailed it** ☐

L'orientation / *Career paths*

Dans quel secteur voudrais-tu travailler?	*In which area would you like to work?*
l'audiovisuel et les médias	*audiovisual and media*
l'informatique et les télécommunications	*IT and telecommunications*
l'hôtellerie et la restauration	*hotel and catering*
les arts et la culture	*arts and culture*
le commerce	*business*
le sport et les loisirs	*sport and leisure*
la médecine et la santé	*medicine and health*
les sciences et les technologies	*science and technology*
Ça m'intéresserait de travailler dans …	*I would be interested in working in …*
Mon rêve serait de faire carrière dans …	*My dream would be to have a career in …*
Mon ambition/Mon but est de trouver un poste dans …	*My ambition/aim is to find a job in …*

Had a look ☐ **Nearly there** ☐ **Nailed it** ☐

Le secteur/L'orientation qui m'attire/m'intéresse (le plus), c'est …	*The sector/career path that attracts/interests me (the most) is …*
L'important pour moi est d'avoir un métier bien payé.	*The important thing for me is to have a well-paid job.*
Le plus important est de …	*The most important thing is to …*
faire quelque chose de satisfaisant/stimulant/ gratifiant/d'intéressant	*do something satisfying/ stimulating/rewarding/ interesting*
faire quelque chose pour améliorer la société/aider les autres	*do something to improve society/help others*
Le salaire a moins d'importance/est très important pour moi.	*The salary is less/very important to me.*
À mon avis, c'est un secteur d'avenir.	*In my opinion, it's an area with prospects.*
Je suis … depuis (trois) ans.	*I have been a … for (three) years.*
C'est un métier (stimulant).	*It's a (stimulating) job.*

Had a look ☐ **Nearly there** ☐ **Nailed it** ☐

La chose qui me plaît le plus, c'est …	*What I like best is …*
L'inconvénient, c'est que …	*The disadvantage is that …*
les horaires sont très longs	*the hours are very long*
c'est fatigant	*it's tiring*

Module 7 Vocabulaire

Le mieux/pire, c'est …	The best/worst thing is …	**Au téléphone**	**On the telephone**
Je suis assez satisfait(e) de mon travail.	I'm quite satisfied with my job.	Allô?	Hello?
Avant, j'étais/je travaillais comme …	In the past, I was/worked as …	Je voudrais parler avec …	I would like to talk to …
C'était affreux/stressant/mieux/pire.	It was awful/stressful/better/worse.	Sa ligne est occupée.	His/Her line is busy.
C'était mal payé.	It was badly paid.	Est-ce que je peux laisser un message?	Can I leave a message?
Le travail était monotone.	The work was monotonous.	Je vais vous transférer vers sa messagerie vocale.	I will transfer you to his/her voicemail.
Il n'y avait aucune possibilité d'avancement.	There was no chance of promotion.	Ne quittez pas.	Stay on the line.
		Je vous le passe.	I'll pass you over to him/her.
Je m'entendais mal avec mon patron.	I didn't get on well with my boss.	Je peux vous être utile?	Can I help you/be of help?
J'ai décidé de (suivre une formation).	I decided to (take a course).	Au revoir!	Goodbye!
Maintenant, je suis diplômé(e).	Now I am qualified.	Had a look ☐ Nearly there ☐ Nailed it ☐	
Mon nouveau boulot est (plus créatif).	My new job is (more creative).	**Un entretien d'embauche**	**A job interview**
Mes collègues sont tous très sympa.	My colleagues are all very nice.	Enchanté(e).	Pleased to meet you.
		Asseyez-vous.	Sit down.
Had a look ☐ Nearly there ☐ Nailed it ☐		Parlez-moi un peu de ce que vous faites actuellement.	Talk to me a little bit about what you are doing at the moment.
Les ambitions	**Ambitions**	Actuellement, je suis (au lycée).	At the moment, I am (in sixth form college).
Avant de continuer mes études, …	Before I continue my studies …	Je suis en train de (préparer le baccalauréat/mes examens de GCSE).	I am in the middle of (preparing to take my baccalauréat/my GCSE exams).
Après avoir terminé mes examens, …	After having finished my exams …		
Après avoir quitté le collège, …	After having left school …	Quelles matières étudiez-vous?	What subjects are you studying?
Plus tard/Un jour, …	Later on/One day …	J'étudie (huit) matières, dont (l'EPS).	I'm studying (eight) subjects, including (PE).
Je veux/J'aimerais/Je préférerais/J'espère	I want/I would like/I would prefer/I hope	Qu'est-ce que vous ferez après vos examens?	What will you do after your exams?
J'ai envie de/d' …	I want to …	Had a look ☐ Nearly there ☐ Nailed it ☐	
J'ai l'intention de/d' …	I intend to …		
Mon rêve serait de/d' …	My dream would be to …	**Mon boulot dans le tourisme**	**My job in tourism**
aller à l'université/à la fac	go to university	Je suis étudiant(e) en …	I am studying …
entrer en apprentissage	do an apprenticeship	J'apprends à devenir …	I'm learning to become …
faire du bénévolat/travail bénévole	do charity/voluntary work	Il y a six mois, j'ai commencé à travailler dans/chez/en …	Six months ago I started work in/with …
prendre une année sabbatique	take a gap year	Je voudrais travailler à plein temps dans (le tourisme).	I would like to work full-time in (tourism).
J'espère me marier/me pacser.	I hope to get married/register a civil partnership.		
J'ai l'intention de faire le tour du monde.	I intend to travel round the world.	Lorsque j'étais plus jeune, je rêvais d'être (infirmier/-ière).	When I was younger, I dreamed of being a (nurse).
Mon but est de fonder une famille.	My aim is to start a family.	J'ai décidé de changer d'orientation à cause de …	I decide to change direction because of …
Je ne veux pas avoir d'enfants.	I don't want to have children.		
Je n'ai aucune intention de m'installer avec mon copain/ma copine.	I have no intention of moving in with my boyfriend/girlfriend.		
Had a look ☐ Nearly there ☐ Nailed it ☐			

Module 7 Vocabulaire

Mon travail consiste à (accueillir les clients).	My work involves (welcoming clients).
Je m'occupe aussi (des réservations).	I also take care of (reservations).

Had a look ☐ **Nearly there** ☐ **Nailed it** ☐

Je vends (des billets).	I sell (tickets).
Je suis passionné(e) par mon travail.	I am passionate about my job.
J'apprécie surtout (le contact avec les gens).	I particularly enjoy (dealing with people).
Le seul inconvénient de mon métier, c'est que …	The only disadvantage of my job is that …
Pour faire ce métier, il faut …	To do this job you have to …
être souriant	smile
savoir parler d'autres langues	know how to speak other languages
Plus tard/Quand je serai diplômé(e), …	Later on/When I am qualified …
je partirai en vacances	I will go on holiday
j'essaierai d'apprendre le japonais	I will try to learn Japanese

Had a look ☐ **Nearly there** ☐ **Nailed it** ☐

Module 7 Vocabulaire

Extra words I should know for reading and listening activities

Le travail	***Work***
l'hôtellerie (f)	*hotel business*
la restauration	*catering*
l'orientation (f)	*careers advice*
l'horaire (m)	*timetable*
la possibilité	*possibility*
la formation	*training*
le boulot	*job*
l'année sabbatique (f)	*sabbatical/gap year*
la licence	*degree*
la sécurité	*security*
le respect	*respect*
la maîtrise	*expertise*
l'inconvénient (m)	*disadvantage*
la lettre de motivation	*covering letter*
l'encadrement (m)	*training*
la fac	*uni*

Had a look ☐ **Nearly there** ☐ **Nailed it** ☐

Les descriptions des emplois	***Work-related descriptions***
diplômé(e)	*qualified*
stimulant(e)	*stimulating*
ancien(e)*	*former, ancient*
pire	*worse*
mal payé(e)	*badly paid*
monotone	*monotonous*
affreux/-euse	*awful*
enrichissant(e)	*enriching*

de mauvaise humeur	*in a bad mood*
créatif/-ve	*creative*
autonome	*independent*
apprenti(e)	*trainee, apprentice*
moi-même	*myself*
à plein temps	*full-time*

Had a look ☐ **Nearly there** ☐ **Nailed it** ☐

Les activités au travail	***Work-related activities***
se débrouiller	*to cope, to manage*
garantir	*to guarantee*
remplir	*to fill*
s'adapter à	*to adapt to*
s'organiser	*to get organised*
entraîner	*to train*
accueillir	*to welcome*
prendre en charge	*to take charge*
animer	*to lead/facilitate activities*
s'occuper de	*to look after*
garder les enfants	*to babysit*
Que faire?	*What do I do?*
poser sa candidature	*to apply for (a job)*
après avoir/être + past participle**	*after having …*

Had a look ☐ **Nearly there** ☐ **Nailed it** ☐

⭐ *Remember that some adjectives like *ancien* change their meaning depending on where they go in relation to the noun.

Examples:

un ancien collège a former school

une ville ancienne an ancient town

⭐ **Use this structure to add a different dimension to your phrases in the past tense.

Example:

Après avoir posé ma candidature … After having applied for my job …

Remember to agree the past participle with the subject when using *être*.

Après être rentrée à la maison, la femme a ouvert les fenêtres. After having returned home, the woman opened the windows.

Module 8 Vocabulaire

Words I should know for speaking and writing activities

Ce qui me préoccupe / What worries me

Ce qui est important pour moi dans la vie, c'est d'abord …	The most important thing to me in life is above all …
Ensuite, c'est …	Then it's …
le sport	sport
la musique	music
ma santé	my health
ma famille	my family
l'argent (m)	money
mes études	my studies
mes animaux	my pets
mes amis	my friends
Ce qui me préoccupe/ m'inquiète (le plus), c'est …	What worries me (the most) is …
l'état (m) de la Terre	the state of the Earth
le réchauffement climatique	global warming
la pauvreté dans le monde	world poverty
l'injustice (f)	injustice
l'environnement (m)	the environment
les sans-abri	homeless people
les personnes qui sont emprisonnées à tort	people who have been wrongly imprisoned
les enfants qui n'ont pas à manger	starving children

Had a look ☐ Nearly there ☐ Nailed it ☐

On peut/Il est possible de …	You can/It's possible to …
parrainer un enfant en Afrique	sponsor a child in Africa
faire un don à une association caritative	donate to a charity
faire du bénévolat	do voluntary work
Il faut …	We must …
lutter contre la faim	fight against hunger/famine
lancer des pétitions	launch petitions
écrire à son/sa député(e)	write to our MP
participer à des manifestations	take part in demonstrations
agir maintenant	act now
faire des campagnes de sensibilisation	carry out campaigns to raise awareness
Il ne faut pas ignorer (ces gens).	We must not ignore (these people).

Had a look ☐ Nearly there ☐ Nailed it ☐

Notre planète / Our planet

Le plus grand problème pour la planète, c'est …	The greatest problem for the planet is …
le changement climatique	climate change
le déboisement	deforestation
la destruction de la couche d'ozone	the destruction of the ozone layer
la destruction des forêts tropicales	the destruction of tropical rainforests
la disparition des espèces	species dying out
la guerre	war
le manque d'eau douce	the lack of fresh water
la pollution de l'air	air pollution
la sécheresse	drought
la surpopulation	overpopulation
un incendie (m)	a fire
une fuite de pétrole	an oil spill
des inondations (f)	flooding, floods
un tremblement de terre	an earthquake
un typhon	a typhoon

Had a look ☐ Nearly there ☐ Nailed it ☐

Protéger l'environnement / Protecting the environment

Que devrait-on faire pour sauver notre planète?	What should we do to save our planet?
Actuellement, je ne fais pas grand-chose pour protéger l'environnement.	Currently, I don't do much to protect the environment.
Je fais déjà pas mal de choses.	I already do quite a lot.
Je pourrais/On devrait …	I could/We ought to …
trier les déchets	separate the rubbish
faire du compost à la maison	make compost at home
éteindre les appareils électriques et la lumière en quittant une pièce	turn off appliances and the light when leaving a room
baisser le chauffage et mettre un pull	turn down the heating and put on a sweater
utiliser du papier recyclé	use recycled paper
éviter les produits jetables	avoid disposable products
acheter des produits verts	buy green products

Had a look ☐ Nearly there ☐ Nailed it ☐

privilégier les produits bio	where possible, choose organic products
utiliser les transports en commun	use public transport
favoriser le covoiturage	encourage car-sharing

M 8

Module 8 Vocabulaire

aller au collège à vélo	go to school by bike
refuser les sacs en plastique	turn down plastic bags
apporter une bouteille d'eau au lieu de prendre un gobelet jetable	carry a bottle of water instead of using disposable cups
récupérer l'eau de pluie pour arroser le jardin	collect rainwater for watering the garden
fermer le robinet pendant qu'on se lave les dents	turn off the tap when cleaning teeth
boire l'eau du robinet	drink tap water
prendre une douche au lieu de prendre un bain	shower instead of taking a bath
tirer la chasse d'eau moins fréquemment	flush the toilet less frequently
faire plus	do more

Had a look ☐ **Nearly there** ☐ **Nailed it** ☐

D'où vient ton tee-shirt? / Where does your T-shirt come from?

Les produits pas chers sont souvent fabriqués dans des conditions de travail inacceptables.	Cheap products are often made in unacceptable working conditions.
Les ouvriers sont sous-payés.	The workers are underpaid.
Leur journée de travail est trop longue.	Their working day is too long.
Si un produit est bon marché, je ne l'achète pas.	If a product is cheap, I don't buy it.
Trop de travailleurs sont exploités/exposés à des risques.	Too many workers are exploited/exposed to risks.

Had a look ☐ **Nearly there** ☐ **Nailed it** ☐

À mon avis, on devrait …	In my opinion, people should …
boycotter les grandes marques qui ne respectent pas leurs ouvriers	boycott big brands that don't respect their workers
forcer les grandes marques à garantir un salaire minimum	force big brands to guarantee a minimum wage
acheter des habits issus du commerce équitable	buy fairly traded clothes
acheter des vêtements fabriqués en France	buy clothes made in France
réfléchir à l'impact sur l'environnement	think about the impact on the environment
essayer de respecter l'homme et l'environnement à la fois	try to respect mankind and the environment at the same time

Had a look ☐ **Nearly there** ☐ **Nailed it** ☐

Faire du bénévolat / Volunteering

Ça me permet d'élargir mes compétences.	It allows me to expand my skills.
Ça me donne plus confiance en moi.	It gives me more confidence in myself/ makes me feel more confident.
Ça me donne le sentiment d'être utile.	It makes me feel useful.
C'est important de participer à la vie en société.	It's important to participate in society.
On a la responsabilité d'aider les autres et de ne pas se focaliser sur soi-même.	We have a responsibility to help others and not focus on ourselves.
Je travaille …	I work …
sur un stand d'Oxfam	on an Oxfam stand
dans un refuge pour les animaux	in an animal sanctuary
Je fais partie de l'organisation X.	I'm a member of X.
Je rends visite à une personne âgée.	I visit an elderly person.
Je participe à des projets de conservation.	I take part in conservation projets.
J'aide des enfants du primaire à faire leurs devoirs.	I help primary school children to do their homework.
Je soigne les animaux.	I look after/treat animals.
Je soutiens les SDF.	I support homeless people.
On s'adresse aux …	We appeal to …
sensibiliser	to raise awareness
prendre conscience de	to become aware of
soigner	to look after, to treat
accueillir	to welcome
affronter	to face, to confront
soutenir	to support

Had a look ☐ **Nearly there** ☐ **Nailed it** ☐

Les grands événements / Big events

Un avantage de cet événement, c'est que …	An advantage of this event is that …
D'un côté, ça …	On the one hand, it …
En plus, ça …	What's more/Moreover, it …
met en avant la culture	promotes the culture
met en avant la ville hôte	promotes the host city
crée un sentiment de fierté nationale	creates a sense of national pride
permet aux gens de passer un bon moment	allows people to have a good time

Module 8 Vocabulaire

encourage la pratique du sport	encourages participation in sport
unit les gens	unites people
donne des modèles aux jeunes	gives young people role models
crée du travail	creates jobs
attire des touristes	attracts tourists

Had a look ☐ **Nearly there** ☐ **Nailed it** ☐

Cependant, …	However, …
un inconvénient, c'est que …	a disadvantage is that …
D'un autre côté, …	On the other hand, …
Par ailleurs, …	What's more, …
les ouvriers qui construisent les stades sont souvent exploités	the workers who build the stadiums are often exploited
les prix augmentent	prices rise
la ville hôte est souvent endettée après l'événement	the host city is often in debt after the event
ça laisse une empreinte carbone très importante	it leaves a major carbon footprint
J'estime/Je trouve/Je suis persuadé(e) que/qu' …	I reckon/find/am persuaded that …
il y a du pour et du contre	there are pros and cons
les festivals sont une chose positive/négative pour un pays/une région	festivals are positive/negative for a country/region
les panneaux solaires	solar panels
les toilettes sèches	dry toilets
les véhicules électriques	electric vehicles
le papier recyclé	recycled paper

Had a look ☐ **Nearly there** ☐ **Nailed it** ☐

M 8

Module 8 Vocabulaire

Extra words I should know for reading and listening activities

Le monde	*The world*
la pauvreté	*poverty*
les déchets (m)	*rubbish*
la surpêche	*overfishing*
l'empreinte carbone (f)	*carbon footprint*
les produits bio (m)	*organic products*
le covoiturage	*car share*
l'hébergement (m)	*accommodation*
l'association caritative (f)	*charity organisation*
les manifestations (f)	*demonstrations*
les pétitions (f)	*petitions*
les conflits (m)	*conflicts*
les campagnes (f)	*campaigns*
la sensibilisation	*raising awareness*
la chasse	*hunting*
les JO (m)	*Olympic games*
les habitants (m)	*inhabitants*
le profile	*profile*
les sans-abri (m)*	*homeless people*
l'appareil électrique (m)	*electrical device*
le chauffage	*heating*
le gobelet	*tumbler*
les bocaux en verre (m)	*glass jars*

Had a look ☐ **Nearly there** ☐ **Nailed it** ☐

Les problèmes et les solutions	*Problems and solutions*
se ficher de	*to not care about something*
réduire	*to reduce*
prendre conscience de	*to become aware of*
se plaindre	*to complain*
abandonner	*to abandon*
souligner	*to underline*
accueillir	*to welcome*
consacrer	*to devote*
faciliter	*to facilitate*
parrainer	*to sponsor*
inquiéter	*to worry*
agir	*to act*
mener	*to lead*
compter	*to count*
entreprendre	*to undertake*
lancer	*to launch*
tourner le dos à qqn	*to turn your back on someone*
donner le bras à qqn	*to give someone a hand*
offrir un café à qqn	*to buy someone a coffee*
donner un coup de poing à qqn	*to hit someone*
requis(e)	*required*
endetté(e)	*indebted*
festivalier	*festival-goer*
en tissu	*made of material/cloth*

Had a look ☐ **Nearly there** ☐ **Nailed it** ☐

Les expressions idiomatiques	*Idioms*
du coup	*as a result, thus*
à la fois	*at the same time*
en fil de fer	*made of wire*
en train de	*in the middle of*
longtemps considéré comme …	*long considered as …*
un milliard	*a billion*
des milliers**	*thousands*

Had a look ☐ **Nearly there** ☐ **Nailed it** ☐

⭐ *Sans* + noun indicates a group of people who do not possess something: homes, legal documents, etc.

Examples:

Les Sans-culottes 'The without breeches' were the common people of the lower classes in late 18th century France, lots of whom fought in the French Revolution in response to their poor quality of life.

Les sans-papiers people without papers/illegal immigrants.

⭐ **Look for words you know already that you see within new words, for example:

mille thousand / *milliers* thousands

ISBN 978-1-292-13242-6